THE ◆ HISTORY ◆ OF
AMERICAN STANDARD

JEFFREY L. RODENGEN

Edited by Alex Lieber
Design and layout by Jill Apolinario and Sandy Cruz

For John Kozyak and Barbara Silverman
who every day set the standard for friendship.

Also by Jeff Rodengen

The Legend of Chris-Craft

*IRON FIST: The Lives
of Carl Kiekhaefer*

*Evinrude-Johnson and
The Legend of OMC*

*Serving The Silent Service:
The Legend of Electric Boat*

The Legend of Dr Pepper/Seven-Up

The Legend of Honeywell

The Legend of Briggs & Stratton

The Legend of Ingersoll-Rand

The MicroAge Way

*The Legend of Stanley:
150 Years of The Stanley Works*

The Legend of Halliburton

The Legend of York International

The Legend of Nucor Corporation

*The Legend of Goodyear:
The First 100 Years*

The Legend of AMP

*Applied Materials:
Pioneering the Information Age*

The Legend of Cessna

The Legend of VF Corporation

The Spirit of AMD

The Legend of Rowan

*New Horizons:
The Story of Ashland Inc.*

The Legend of Federal-Mogul

The Legend of Amdahl

*Connected:
The History of Inter-Tel*

The Legend of Pfizer

The Legend of Echlin

Publisher's Cataloging in Publication

Rodengen, Jeffrey L.
  The history of American Standard /Jeffrey L. Rodengen.
1st ed.
p. cm.
  Includes bibliographical references and index.
  ISBN 0-945903-48-0

1. American Standard, inc. 2. Heating equipment industry.
3. Air conditioning equipment industry. 4. Plumbing equipment
industry. I. Title

HD9683.A6R64 1998   338.7'697
                                      QBI97-41440

Write Stuff Enterprises, Inc.

1515 Southeast 4th Avenue • Fort Lauderdale, FL 33316
1-800-900-Book (1-800-900-2665) • (954) 462-6657

Library of Congress Catalog Card Number 97-62157

ISBN 0-945903-48-0

Completely produced in the United States of America
10 9 8 7 6 5 4 3 2 1

Demand Flow®, is a federally registered trademark of John Costanza Institute of Technology, Inc.

TABLE OF CONTENTS

INTRODUCTION

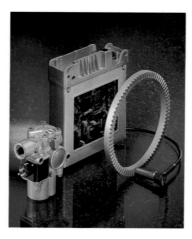

SINCE ITS CREATION BY THE merger of American Radiator and Standard Sanitary Manufacturing in 1929, American Standard has redefined itself several times amid a changing world. Born on the cusp of the Great Depression, the company continues to exhibit the strength and tenacity that has characterized its history for 70 years.

This heating and plumbing pioneer has thrived because the company evolved to meet market conditions all over the world. It never shrank from opportunity or challenge, always striving to improve efficiency. When Clarence Woolley, one of American Radiator's founders, approached Standard Sanitary's Theodore Ahrens in 1928, he had in mind the creation of a one-stop shopping center for the construction industry. The union of the two established an international powerhouse and helped advance the ideals championed by Ahrens — the standardization of plumbing and sanitation equipment and codes to safeguard the public's health. Woolley and Ahrens both took it as an article of faith that their job was to educate the public in the new technologies and materials they knew would revolutionize living conditions around the world.

For many years the union was rocky, but time and again the corporation surmounted internal and external crises, growing internationally and into new markets. With its expanding reservoir of corporate wealth, American Standard acquired a host of companies and product lines as it matured. At one point during the diversification craze of the sixties, American Standard bought as many as 110 companies or product lines. Many were later sold off to cover the immense debt that resulted, but they left the American Standard family in better financial shape than when they were purchased.

American Standard's treatment of subsidiaries gave it a sterling reputation for ethical management. Companies were absorbed without creating unrestrained havoc among management and employees. American Standard's most vital acquisitions, Westinghouse Air Brake Company in 1969 and The Trane Company in 1983, are two of the most enduring examples of American Standard's strategy. WABCO and Trane retained their individual spirits of innovation as well as pride in their historical contributions to the health and comfort of customers all over the globe. Despite a depressed U.S. market in 1938, Reuben Trane, son of Norwegian immigrant James Trane and head of the Trane Company, fervently believed that there was a need for a "modern way" to cool water for the fledgling air conditioning industry.

Trane's solution was the air conditioning industry's first hermetically sealed centrifugal water chiller, the Turbovac®, launched in 1939. Likewise, WABCO, founded by one of America's greatest inventors, George Westinghouse, entered into a unique collaborative partnership with Mercedes Benz to develop new product technologies. In 1981, WABCO introduced the antilock braking system for commercial vehicles with Mercedes Benz becoming its first major customer.

The mettle of American Standard and all of its people was sorely tested when the corporation bled green to thwart a hostile takeover attempt in 1988. Successful but wounded, the company went private and took on a mountain of debt just as a recession was beginning. American Standard had to dig deep within itself to survive. Its leaders bet the company on a new process called Demand Flow® Technology (DFT), unlocking the company's hidden strength in its working capital. DFT turned inventory into cash, sliced production time, improved quality and reduced bureaucracy.

But management and production theories only achieve results when the company's culture has a strong sense of mission, dedication and teamwork. The process was important, but it was the spirit of the organization that made it work. American Standard started off as a disparate and unorganized collection of companies that sometimes worked at cross purposes. Now the walls have been brought down figuratively and literally, as each section works for the greater whole. (Many offices no longer have walls separating the various functions of a unit. In the U.S. Plumbing Group, for instance, one only has to stand in the middle of the room to find someone.)

At the end of the decade, American Standard stands leaner and stronger than it was at the beginning. As it enters the new millennium, the company will continue to overcome challenges, pursuing its mission of manufacturing products to make the world a safer and healthier place in which to live.

FOREWORD

By
Dan Quayle
Former Vice President of the United States of America

ONE DAY, NOT LONG AFTER my election to American Standard's board of directors in 1993, the board was preparing for a trip to England. Just before we left, I looked over my shoulder at our CEO and chairman, Emmanuel Kampouris. He was engaged in an earnest conversation with a line worker. This was about three years after Kampouris had staked American Standard's survival on a new manufacturing process called Demand Flow® Technology. The chairman and CEO considered it vitally important that everyone understood how DFT should work — vice presidents, managers, supervisors, right down to individual line workers.

The look on Mano Kampouris' face told me the worker didn't understand some facet of DFT he should have. In DFT, workers must know more than their own jobs; they must have a clear understanding of the entire manufacturing process after it leaves their station. After talking to the worker, he methodically went back up the ladder of command, making sure each person on each rung not only understood the process, but knew how to convey that knowledge with those around them.

This episode wasn't only about Demand Flow Technology, however, but also about the character of American Standard, which can be summed up in a word — teamwork. Whether in a board room in Piscataway, New Jersey, or on a factory floor in the Chinese province of Guangdong, employees and managers work together to reach our corporate goals across every product line and in every market. The board of directors work closely with Mano to define these goals. He in turn relies on his executive team to develop the strategies to reach new milestones in plumbing, automotive, HVAC and medical systems. In each category American Standard has been a leader in innovation and technology.

Taking calculated risks in technology and strategy is familiar ground for American Standard. Following the 1988 hostile takeover attempt, for example, management took the bold step of privatizing. As a result, the company struggled with a $3.2 billion mountain of debt and a recession that was just beginning. Mano Kampouris courageously navigated the crisis by adopting Demand Flow Technology in 1990. It took leadership and teamwork of all involved to adapt the organization to this new and untried concept, but the results are clear. Five years later, American Standard once again entered the public domain, leaner and stronger than ever before.

But the lesson here is more than taking risks on unproven technology. It is about setting far-reaching goals and striving for success. With the working capital unlocked by DFT, American Standard invested in the research and development of products like the Automotive Group's electronic braking system, the Air Conditioning Group's chiller technology and the Medical Systems Group's Copalis diagnostic device. Joint venture strategies enabled the Plumbing Products to open two of its largest European factories in the Czech Republic and Bulgaria.

And finally, American Standard found the resources to train *every* worker in Demand Flow concepts and techniques. Management realizes that our mission must be understood at every level, and the message has to be translated into many languages so it can be understood by all as American Standard grows.

As a public servant, I have witnessed the stellar achievements realized when people pull together and work toward a shared vision. Team spirit is too often dismissed as cliché, but it is in fact a working concept vital to a company as global and as diverse in cultures and product lines as American Standard. Mano Kampouris is the forward-thinking engineer of American Standard's continuing success. His restless energy revitalized the company, and his leadership brought American Standard back to public ownership, where it can continue to serve in the public's best interests. As we enter the new millennium and an increasingly global economy, the challenge remains daunting, but the reward is gratifying. All of us connected with American Standard share the genuine feeling of success in the marketplace, and the quiet pride in the knowledge that our products help to ensure both the health and comfort of our customers.

From my vantage point as a board member, I have come to respect American Standard's leadership, innovation and willingness to communicate with itself and with customers. For no matter what the formula or structure, the success of any enterprise comes down to its people.

Dan Quayle's life in the public sector began in 1971 when he became an investigator for the Consumer Protection Division of the Indiana Attorney General's Office. In 1976, at age 29, he was elected to the U.S. Congress, defeating an eight-term incumbent Democrat. In 1980, a 33-year-old Quayle made Indiana political history by becoming the youngest person from that state to win a seat to the U.S. Senate, defeating a three-term Democrat. He won reelection six years later by the widest margin in Indiana history. As senator, Quayle served on prominent committees, including the Armed Service and Budget committees. He helped author the successful Job Training Partnership Act, which has been called one of the most important pieces of social legislation passed during the Reagan Administration.

In 1988, Quayle joined George Bush on the Republican presidential ticket and was elected vice president of the United States at age 41. One of the most active vice presidents in American history, Quayle made official visits to 47 nations. At home, Quayle advocated a strong national defense, legal reform, deregulation and a return to basic American values. He continues to encourage personal responsibility, entrepreneurship, limited government and the importance of faith.

ACKNOWLEDGMENTS

RESEARCHING, WRITING AND publishing *The History of American Standard* would not have been possible without the effort and guidance of a great many individuals, both inside and outside the company.

First of all, I would like to thank my research assistant Jennifer Salvato. Jennifer conducted much of the initial research and original timelines for the book. I would also like to thank Ed Wencek, retired records administrator, for his diligent collection of images and documents of American Standard's history.

Particular gratitude is extended to Lisa Glover, director of corporate communications for American Standard and Adrian Deshotel, vice president of corporate human resources. Their guidance and enthusiasm for the project provided a source of inspiration. I am also especially grateful to Chairman and CEO Emmanuel Kampouris, who generously took time from his busy schedule to contribute to the project. Special thanks goes to Vice Chairman Horst Hinrichs and George Kerckhove, vice president and CFO. These men went to great lengths and effort to provide the fascinating histories of WABCO and Trane respectively. I am indebted to William Marquard, retired chairman and CEO of American Standard for his recollections, as well as the recollections of Alan

Root, executive vice president, and the late John Grant, who had retired as vice president of finance and administration.

The candid insights of American Standard executives, both current and retired, were crucial to the book. Among these I would like to thank: Giancarlo Aimetti, vice president, Automotive Products, Austria Group; Fred Allardyce, senior vice president, medical products sector; Alec Apolostolopoulos, vice president and group executive of Plumbing Products, business and product development; the late Frank Berberich, who had retired as vice president; Dr. Judy Britz, vice president, Medical Systems Group; Gary Brogoch, vice president, Plumbing Products, Far East; Robert Cavey, vice president of government and public affairs; Annabelle Christie, assistant to Emmanuel Kampouris; Robert Crooks, retired chief patent counsel; Wilfried Delker, vice president and group executive, Plumbing Products (worldwide fittings); Joe DeSantis, vice president of sales (wholesale channel), U.S. Plumbing Products; David De Wahl, retired general counsel and corporate secretary; John Donnelly, former counsel; Fabio Lunghi, former vice president, Medical Systems Group; Don Feigel, retired member of sales and distribution team; Cyril Gallimore, retired vice president, Systems and Technology; Luigi Gandini, vice president, Special Projects; John Geer, retired general counsel; David Gleditsch, DFT formalization leader; Barbara Glenn, retired assistant to William Marquard; John Grant, retired senior vice president; Herb Hadley, retired director, benefits; Hugh Hoffman, process owner for chinaware order fulfillment, U.S. Plumbing Products; Fred Jaqua, retired vice president and general counsel; Wayne Jolliffe, vice president, human resources for the U.S. Plumbing Group; Richard Kalaher, vice president, general counsel and secretary; Craig Kissel, senior vice president, Automotive Group; William Klug, retired vice president and group executive, Air Conditioning Products; Robert Levinson, former group vice president and a founder of Steelcraft; Sandy MacGregor, retired corporate counsel; Janet Murnick, former vice president, Medical Systems Group; Eric Nutter, vice president and group executive, Plumbing Products Americas; David Pannier, vice president, vice president and group executive, Air Conditioning Products, North American Unitary Group; Raymond Pipes, vice president, investor relations; Erich Reinecke, vice president of engineering, Automotive Products; Roy Satchell, retired senior vice president, security and graphics; James Schultz, vice president, group executive, Air Conditioning Products, Worldwide Applied Systems Group; Benson Stein, vice president of operations, Medical Systems Group; Henry Steiner, retired vice president and tax counsel; Angela Tripodi, executive assistant; Robert Wellbrock, vice president, taxes; Colin Wise, retired vice president, finance; Carl Zeigler, retired pricing administrator; Hans Zinzow, retired controller; Wolfgang Voss, vice president, Automotive Products.

I would also like to thank John Costanza, founder, president and CEO of JCIT, for explaining the Demand Flow process, and the courage and dedication with which American Standard embraced this new method. Frank Nickell, president of Kelso & Company, was particularly informative in describing the relationship of trust between American Standard and Kelso during the hostile takeover period.

I am especially grateful to Dan Quayle, former vice president of the United States, and a member of American Standard's board of directors. Mr. Quayle thoughtfully provided the foreword for the book.

Special thanks goes to Art Scheskie, director of for The Trane Company, who went above and beyond the call by contributing rare images to help illustrate the chapter on Trane. I would also like to thank Guy Aceto, of *Air Force Magazine*, for once again coming through with images on short notice.

And finally, a very special word of thanks to the dedicated staff at Write Stuff. Proofreader Bonnie Freeman and transcriptionist Mary Aaron worked quickly and efficiently. Indexer Mary Redgate assembled this comprehensive index. Particular gratitude goes to Alex Lieber, executive editor; Catherine Lackner, Melody Maysonet and Jon VanZile, associate editors; Sandy Cruz and Jill Apolinario, art directors; Fred Moll, production manager; Colleen Azcona and Jill Thomas, assistants to the author; Marianne Roberts, office manager; Ivan Bial, sales and promotions manager; Bonnie Bratton, director of marketing; Rafael Santiago, logistics specialist; and Karine Rodengen, project coordinator.

A bas-relief created for American Radiator's presentation at the 1904 St. Louis World's Fair. The relief was described as "an allegorical study."

CHAPTER ONE

AMERICAN RADIATOR–
THE FIRST HEAT WAVE
1872–1929

"The men who grew up with American Radiator Company, and saw the Industry prosper with its growth, were characterized by their devotion and love for the Company. Through every anxiety and every triumph the emotions and thoughts of these men were united in a single effort and desire."

— Clarence M. Woolley, 1929[1]

AMERICAN RADIATOR COMPANY can trace its roots to 1872, the year John B. Pierce decided to buy a tinware shop. Pierce was a young man in search of opportunity. He left home at 16 and spent two years working in a drugstore, four years at a Wisconsin lumber firm and another four at a New Hampshire stove and furnace business. After an unsuccessful attempt to move to the Northwest in 1871, a discouraged Pierce returned East, as he later recounted.

"For want of something more and better to do, I took the train early in January and arrived in Ware [Massachusetts] one cold, bleak winter day about 6 p.m., went to the hotel for supper and later crossed the street to the little shop I came to see. I looked in at the window and saw the proprietor figuring on a slate by the light of a tallow candle, the only light in the store, which as I remember was about 20 feet by 60 feet."[2]

Pierce learned the tin shop was for sale. The shop's proprietor was an honest man. He admitted that the business was in financial trouble. Undeterred, Pierce began negotiating. The shop owner offered to sell for $2,800; Pierce countered with a $2,500 cash offer. When the owner declined, Pierce returned to Boston and "never expected to see Ware again." But a few days later the young entrepreneur, anxious to get to work on something, met the $2,800 asking price.[3]

Pierce took over the small shop on January 8, 1872, and began renovating it. He cleaned the windows, straightened out the stock, added large hanging lamps and gave the place a fresh coat of paint. "The change created so much of a sensation that one or two customers came in, not to buy anything in particular, but to see what the trouble was, and learn the cause of so much commotion."[4]

That same year Pierce hired 19-year-old Joseph Bond, a young man who walked into the shop looking for work. At the time, Bond had a job, earning $3 a day, but was eager to get involved in a new business venture even if it meant taking a pay cut. Pierce liked the young man's style and hired him on the spot. During his first year with Pierce, Bond earned only $350, but the two men embarked on a lifelong friendship.

After they had been in business together for a year, Pierce sold his interest in the Ware shop to

John B. Pierce, founder of the Pierce Steam Heating Company in Buffalo, New York.

The first home of the Pierce Steam Heating Company, in Buffalo, New York. John Pierce and Joseph Bond built the plant with second-hand lumber for $500.

Bond and left for Buffalo, leaving the young man to build a successful enterprise on his own. Pierce was looking for yet another business venture and planned to send for Bond as soon as he found it.

The Panic of 1873 delayed his plans. After the Civil War, railroads had accelerated their push to the West, expanding into some areas that proved unprofitable. At the same time, the federal government tightened the money supply. In the summer of 1873, 25 railroads defaulted on loans, creating a ripple effect throughout the financial and investment community, causing the stock market to close for 10 days and triggering a depression that would last six years.

1872 — John Pierce buys a tinware shop in Massachusetts and hires Joseph Bond.

1887 — Clarence Woolley joins Michigan Radiator & Iron Company.

1872

1881 — Pierce and Bond begin the Pierce Steam Heating Company in Buffalo, New York.

1892 — Woolley helps merge three companies to form American Radiator Company.

The nation's economy eventually rebounded at a time when America's population was growing rapidly. Farm production had doubled despite the fact that many people were forsaking family farms to move to cities, and railroads began expanding once again. Driven by the industrial revolution, manufacturing grew at a phenomenal rate.

Buoyed by these positive signs, Pierce founded the Pierce Steam Heating Company in 1881 and asked Bond to join him in Buffalo, New York. They manufactured steel boilers and, eventually, radiators — a new form of heating that was quickly replacing the old method of heating buildings with hot water and steam pipes.

By the mid-1800s, radiators (a series of pipe castings through which boiler-generated steam is forced) came into use, but the search for inexpensive, reliable heat wasn't over. Only the affluent could afford to purchase a system of steel radiators, boilers and furnaces to centrally heat their homes. Steel radiators remained beyond the reach of the average person.

It was not until the invention of the cast-iron radiator in 1886 that clean, efficient home heating became affordable. Demand for cast-iron radiators grew quickly, and the Pierce Steam Heating Company flourished. By the end of the 1880s, the Buffalo manufacturing plant could barely keep up with orders.[5]

With the help of a man named Clarence M. Woolley, the overburdened Pierce Steam Heating Company merged with Michigan Radiator & Iron and Detroit Radiator, creating a giant in the radiator and steam-heat market. Woolley was general manager of Michigan Radiator, a company in the forefront of the new cast-iron process.

Detroit Radiator was the first to use the cast-iron process, but Michigan Radiator quickly adopted the process with a twist: Woolley drove down costs by building the product in sections rather than in one piece, which allowed him to custom-design its dimensions.

Clarence Mott Woolley

Clarence Woolley was born September 15, 1863, in Detroit. Like Bond and Pierce, Woolley was a self-made man who made the most of every opportunity. His father, Smith Woolley, had been a wealthy Detroit banker and iron manufacturer who lost his fortune in the depression of 1873. Until the collapse, Clarence Woolley was being

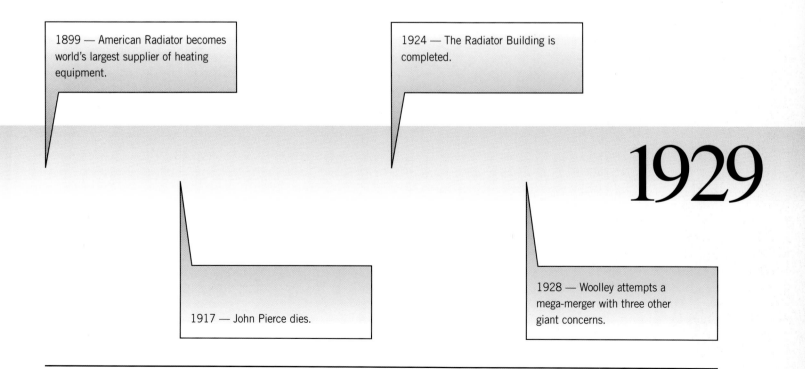

1899 — American Radiator becomes world's largest supplier of heating equipment.

1924 — The Radiator Building is completed.

1929

1917 — John Pierce dies.

1928 — Woolley attempts a mega-merger with three other giant concerns.

Clarence Mott Woolley worked his way up from a $5-a-week office boy to the general manager of Michigan Radiator before helping to engineer the merger forming American Radiator.

when Michigan Radiator, Detroit Radiator and the Pierce Steam Heating Company merged to form American Radiator Company in 1892.

Woolley recognized his limitations; supervising corporate mergers at that time was one of them. He tracked down Adolphus Williamson Green, the Chicago lawyer who orchestrated the merger that eventually led to Nabisco Brands, Inc. (Nabisco was born from the merger of the New York Biscuit Company and the American Biscuit Company in 1898.) For $100 plus expenses, Green put together American Radiator Company.

At the time of the merger, the combined earnings of the three companies was $300,000. Bond became president; Pierce, vice president; Charles Hodges (who had headed Detroit Radiator), treasurer; and Woolley, secretary. Headquartered in Chicago, American Radiator was capitalized at $3 million of preferred assets and $5 million of common stock.

Merging the companies wasn't easy, as Pierce later wrote.

"Some of you do not know, and cannot comprehend the chaos that existed in this organization, or rather disorganization, January 1, '92. ... You would never believe that such a beautiful whole had been conceived and brought forth, from such a confusion of parts. It was like bringing together of the multitudinous parts of three different machines."[6]

groomed to attend Andover and Yale, and was forced to shift from a private grammar school to a public one. When his father died several years later, 15-year-old Clarence quit school altogether to find work.

Hired by a wholesale crockery firm, Fisk and Company, the ambitious Woolley began his career as a $5-a-week office boy. He worked 12 hours a day, six days a week, rising to become a salesman. After eight years, the 23-year-old Woolley was named general manager. On the advice of a family friend, Woolley approached the managers of Michigan Radiator & Iron Company in 1887.

Woolley joined the company as head of sales. By the age of 28 he had become general manager of the company and was the primary facilitator

The transition may have been rocky, but in its first year, American Radiator did well, netting about $400,000 in income. But the failure of the Philadelphia & Reading Railroad and a panic on Wall Street touched off the depression of 1893, the worst then on record. Millions lost their jobs as labor and management became locked in bitter battles throughout the country. By 1894 more than 750,000 workers had gone on strike.

American Radiator was able to keep its Detroit and Buffalo plants open by gambling on the European market. A German engineer had suggested to Woolley that his company could do well in Europe, so although the company had virtually no profits at that point, Woolley decided he could make a sales trip overseas for about $800.[7] Arriving in Paris, Woolley learned from a business associate that the Swiss government was building a new capital building. "I lost no time in reaching Berne and getting in touch with Heinrich Berchtold, the heating contractor," he later recorded.[8]

Over a luncheon with the Swiss engineer, Berchtold, Woolley struck a $50,000 deal to supply 30 carloads of cast-iron radiators for the Swiss capital building under construction.[9] When Bond and Hodges heard about the deal, they refused to believe it. Woolley cabled them with confirmation of the order. He cabled again with more surprises:

"On receipt of this vast order, so considered in those days, my fellow executives, Mr. Bond and Mr. Hodges, cabled me to ask if I was serious or if it was a joke. I cabled that it was a real order and for them to present shipping receipts to the banking house of Iselin & Company, New York, receiving cash on receipt of said documents. ... Thus was the first order obtained in Europe.

"After finishing the job in Switzerland I proceeded to Hamburg where Rude Otto Meyer Company gave me several large orders for the new City Hall and for other important buildings. They proved to be the largest and most important company in Europe, and our relations continued for many years thereafter. They were scientific installers of heating apparatus."[10]

Woolley also obtained orders in France and Belgium. By 1895 the growth of export sales made it inefficient to manufacture radiators for Europe in Buffalo or Detroit. This time it was Bond who made a trip overseas to set up an English branch, with headquarters in London. The first big order in England was to supply radiators for post offices in Great Britain. The foreign market grew to be one of Woolley's many areas of expertise, and he continued to make yearly trips to search for opportunity.

As the economy recovered in 1897, American Radiator purchased Britain's Ideal Boiler Company and began manufacturing round cast-iron boilers as well as sectional and square boilers. The following year American Radiator set up another foreign subsidiary, this time in France.

A Wave of Consolidation

In 1899, with the help of legendary financier J.P. Morgan, American Radiator brought virtually the entire heating equipment industry under the American Radiator name.[11] Morgan helped engineer many conglomerates in the belief that competitors should combine for greater efficiency. His greatest accomplishment would be, of course, the formation of the United States Steel Corporation in 1901.

The company consolidated with St. Louis Radiator Company of St. Louis, Missouri; Standard Radiator Company of Buffalo, New York; Model Radiator of Elwood, Indiana; Holland Radiator of Bremen, Indiana; and M. Steel Company of Springfield, Ohio.

Although the consolidation pales in comparison to earlier and later mergers engineered by Morgan, American Radiator had become the world's largest supplier of heating equipment by the dawn of the 20th century. (Edison General Electric and Thomson-Houston General Electric formed General Electric in

American Radiator Company's cast-iron process enabled it to fashion radiators to customers' specifications. This Detroit Ornamental Fluted radiator, for example, could be made to fit any desired pitch of stairs.

PERSISTENCE PAYS

JOSEPH BOND, JOHN PIERCE'S partner and salesman, was known for his tenacity. C.S. Hopkins, a contractor, related a story that revealed not only Bond's determination, but also his graciousness.

"In the spring of 1882, I was at Canandaigua, New York, in the hardware store of Mr. Theodore Perkins, when I noticed an advertisement with an illustration of the Pierce Boiler. I wrote and requested a catalogue on Mr. Perkins' letterhead. A day or two later, Mr. Bond called at Mr. Perkins' store with my letter in his hand. Mr. Perkins told him that I had just left for Rochester, and that I had said I would call on a Dr. Wolters." [1]

Bond took the train to Rochester "and hunted high and low for a Dr. Walters," Hopkins said. Before realizing his error, "he called on four different Walterses (remember, this was before the days of telephones!)." [2]

"Finally, locating Dr. Wolters, he learned that I had been there but had left for Lockport, New York, and that I usually stopped at the Holly Company Shop. Having an hour to wait for a train, Mr. Bond proceeded to sell Dr. Wolters a boiler! Mr. Bond then took the train to Lockport, arriving at about 5 p.m. He went immediately to the Holly Company Shop. I had been there and left, but he was told that I always stopped at a boarding house on Locust Street. When I reached the boarding house about 6:30 p.m., Bond was waiting for me. He finally had run me to earth." [3]

The two had supper together and talked shop, Hopkins said. "I felt very much flattered as he asked me question after question, as though he was gratified to have reached the fountain of wisdom relating to steam heating. Was he a diplomat? I would say he was! I was puffed up to the skies. Years afterwards, I wondered if he had had a quiet laugh over the green young fellow who thought he knew it all.

"But as I knew him better, I realized that his kindly nature was prompting him to encourage a young man." [4]

Above: The Detroit Dining Room radiator served as a dish- or food-warmer in well-appointed dining rooms.

Right: Waking up to winter is never a pleasure without heat.

"We are pleased to report that the latter source of demand is becoming more important and formidable as publicity is given to the economy and healthfulness of steam and hot water systems of heating. The general public is rapidly learning the sanitary advantages and the fuel economy of modern heating methods, which constantly develops an expanding field of demand."[12]

American Radiator's advertising in 1904 highlighted the comfort and safety provided by the company's products.

"Winter's Dread is the bed-time thought of rising, dressing, bathing and breakfasting in cold rooms. There's a way out. American Radiators & Ideal Boilers keep the house uniformly warm in the morning — all day in any kind of weather — without attention to the fire during the night. ... Family Health is Protected."[13]

1891; Carnegie Steel Company and others formed the United States Steel Corporation, the first billion-dollar corporation, in 1901.)

Net profits in 1900 reached an impressive $1.2 million, but by 1902 — when Bond died and the 39-year-old Woolley took over as company president — that number more than doubled to $2.5 million. In 1902, the company also completed a new plant in Buffalo, named the Bond Plant. American Radiator also built a new plant in Germany and enlarged the factory in France.

The company's 1903 Annual Report attributed American Radiator's growth to a surge in new construction and the introduction of its products into existing buildings.

Winter's Dread is the bed-time thought of rising, dressing, bathing and breakfasting in cold rooms. There's a way out.

AMERICAN RADIATORS & IDEAL BOILERS

keep the house uniformly warm in the morning—all day—any kind of weather—without attention to the fire during the night. When you recall the fuel needlessly burned or the discomforts caused last winter by old fashioned methods, why wait longer to ask about our way of steam or water warming your home? The fuel saving—the cleanliness—absence of repairs—pay in time for the outfit. *Family health is protected.*

Simple to put into *old* cottages, houses, buildings, etc. Easy to run as a parlor stove. No street water supply required. Put in now at *summer* prices by best mechanics. Ask for booklet.

AMERICAN RADIATOR COMPANY

We manufacture 36 different regular patterns and 67 odd shapes of radiators to fit any space or location in the rooms.

Dept. CHICAGO

The general offices of American Radiator's French subsidiary, located in Paris.

American Radiator's patents gave it a monopoly on the cast-iron market in the early years. But Woolley was not content to rely on existing patents — he emphasized research for continued growth. He would not be satisfied, for instance, until American Radiator developed and delivered the first completely rigid or "screw nipple" radiator, which provided better connection between the sections to prevent leakage.

In 1907 business took another downturn, but the company was ready. Keeping a close eye on economic indicators, Woolley made sure American Radiator's inventory was low and bought pig iron on a day-to-day basis.

"The company passed through the panic of 1907 without stress or strain and emerged therefrom with cash on hand approximately equal to its liabilities. ... The inventories of raw materials and manufactured products were adjusted at the end of the year on the basis of actual market values, by utilization of funds reserved for that purpose."[14]

Later that year, the company opened a Canadian subsidiary and within two years expanded to Italy, Austria and Belgium.

The War to End All Wars

As American Radiator prospered at home and overseas, war clouds gathered over Europe. By 1914, the tinder-dry alliances of Germany and Great Britain required only a spark to ignite the world's first mechanized war. The assassination of the Austrian Archduke Francis Ferdinand and his wife Sophie by a Serbian terrorist provided the spark. One by one, nations joined in the "Great War," which pitted the Central Powers (chiefly Germany and Austria-Hungary) against the Allies (chiefly Great Britain, France and Russia).

By 1915, with both sides bogged down within cold, miserable trenches, it was clear the war would not soon end. Prices of pig iron kept rising, and the astute Woolley decided to purchase 100,000 tons at a reasonable $15 a ton in Europe. By the time the United States entered the war in 1917, the price had soared to $40 a ton.

In 1914, on the eve of the war, Clarence Woolley had decided to go abroad to gather first-hand information about the company's plants and offices in England and on the European continent. He wrote extensive letters of his experiences prior to and following the outbreak of the war.

Arriving in France, Woolley was captivated by the unfolding drama. On August 3, 1914 (the day Germany declared war on France), he praised the "calmness, the confidence and the poise of the French people at this critical hour ... for in this supreme moment they quietly move along, each fulfilling his part in the great drama."[15]

Several days before hostilities, Woolley and his traveling companions had withdrawn a sizable sum of cash from European banks. "Had we not taken this precaution," he wrote home to his board of directors, "we would be in a very dangerous position, for the banks are refusing to pay out any money whatsoever. We shall apply this money in driblets as the occasion shall require it ... but shall not indulge in cablegrams except when necessary, for we think it proper to economize in this respect."

Only 26 of the French company's 95 men — "boys, English or those disqualified by disability" — had not joined the army. "We said 'au revoir' to each man this morning, and while the parting was not enthusiastic ... each man indicated a certain alertness and resolution," Woolley wrote. Eventually the plant was converted to military barracks.

Even at that late date people still hoped war could be averted, wrote Woolley.

AFRICA

"Everyone would hail with delight the news that the impending conflict could be settled by diplomacy, ... the German ambassador has not yet left Paris nor has the French ambassador departed from Berlin. It would be a miracle if the war could now be prevented, but occasionally one hears the hope that something may happen in the next few hours."[16]

The naval arms race between Great Britain and Germany, and the latter's desire for recognition as a world power, made the conflict inevitable. Woolley was one of the few who recognized that this conflict would entail carnage on a scale never seen before.

Woolley left for London. "We found the affairs of the English company in excellent condition," he wrote on September 18, 1914. "Mr. Shearer has exhibited splendid judgment in directing its course during these unprecedented times." Radiator sales were about 20 percent lower than the previous year, but Woolley attributed that to the declining export business. (The English company had exported a considerable number of radiators to war-torn Belgium.) Boiler sales, however, had declined by only 10 percent.

Woolley also gathered first-hand information about what Europeans believed would be the long-term financial effect of the war. He read articles in European publications and spoke with bankers and "well-informed persons," arriving at the conclusion that the war would not last long, and when it was over there would be an economic rebound from which companies like American Radiator could benefit. Woolley also reported on the state of the German plants and offices.

"A large percentage of the office people at Berlin promptly were called to the Colors at the outbreak of the war, but enough remained to

Above right: The American Radiator logo, circa 1900.

Left: This map shows the location of American Radiator European plants at the outbreak of World War I. Plants located in Austria-Hungary, Germany and Belgium (invaded by Germany early in the war) fell under control of the Central Powers.

transact the comparatively small amount of business which is offered them. The Neuss Plant has been closed down. The construction of the new malleable foundry was abandoned. Schoenebeck Plant is running about one-third of its capacity, and the orders received were somewhat in excess of the output so that the stock is being reduced."[17]

Woolley sailed for home on the SS *Lusitania* October 3, 1914, eight months before the English luxury liner was torpedoed and sent to the bottom of the Atlantic Ocean — along with 1,100 passengers and crew — by a German submarine attack.

President Woodrow Wilson, re-elected under the banner "He Kept Us Out of the War," struggled for neutrality. Strong ties to the Allies, and Germany's unrestricted submarine warfare, led the United States to sever diplomatic ties with Germany. On April 6, 1917, Congress formally declared war.

The nation was unprepared, however, and Wilson created the War Industries Board to allocate scarce materials, standardize

production and prices, and coordinate purchasing. American Radiator largely stopped producing radiators and boilers to meet the needs for war materiel. "Immediately upon our country's declaration of war, the company offered its manufacturing facilities to the Government, and the Navy Department took over the Bayonne Plant in Bayonne, New Jersey, for the manufacture of naval guns under an arrangement which indicates a small profit to the company," Woolley reported to stockholders.[18] In 1917, Woolley was named vice chairman of the War Trade Board in control of all imports and exports.

America's entry into the war coincided with a coal shortage and a bitterly cold winter "so severe that local officials commandeered coal trains passing through their jurisdictions, and policemen had to stand guard over industrial coal piles to prevent pilfering."[19] Conservation became critical, and American Radiator responded with more efficient boiler designs:

"The demand for utilities of highest efficiency, because of the pressing problems of national conservation, is met by this Company through its standard line of heating devices, which induce marked savings in fuel consumption and domestic labor. ... Representative of advanced engineering and utmost fuel conservation is the Ideal Type 'A' Sectional Boiler. ... Through its use the old-time experiences of the 'run-away' fire are to give place to the controlled fire, by means of scientifically measured heating surfaces and automatic regulation."[20]

The company also encouraged buying Liberty Bonds to help fund the war effort. By the end of 1917, the company and employees together had contributed more than $1.1 million to pay for the war.[21] American Radiator also encouraged stock ownership by its employees. In 1917, more than 20 percent of the company was in the hands of its own workers.

Cooperation was the monthly magazine for American Radiator Company's workers. The 1929 issue restated the company's purpose.

A portion of the stock was made available upon the death of one of the company's founders, John Pierce, who died on June 23, 1917. Pierce's will distributed two-thirds of his shares to more than 400 employees and created the John B. Pierce Foundation,

"Whose object shall be the promotion of all or either: research, educational, technical, or scientific work in the general field of heating, ventilation and sanitation, for the increase of knowledge to the end that the general hygiene and comfort of human beings and their habitations may be advanced."[22]

American Radiator also established a Department of Industrial Relations to promote better communication between management and employees. The department administered the usual duties of the modern human resources department, such as employment, welfare and group insurance, and also acted as mediator between the manager and the employee in disputes to make "definite the assurance that each employee receives an absolutely square deal in his every relation with the company."[23]

As the war dragged on, the company's civilian production dropped off as it produced more war materiel. American Radiator manufactured munitions (which produced a small profit margin), 4-inch and 5-inch naval guns and accompanying spare parts, and hand grenades at six plants (Bayonne, Bond, Equipment, Kansas City, Malleable and Pierce).

A more poignant contribution came from the 800 workers who joined the Army or Navy during the conflict. Of those, 16 were killed in action.

Radiator Building: A Legacy

With the end of the war in 1918, the company welcomed back its veterans and returned to civilian production. By 1921, home construction reached record numbers as returning veterans sought homes. Energy-efficient heaters like the Type "A" Boiler, built in response to the wartime energy crunch, sold well even after the pressure of conservation abated. "These Type 'A' machines represent actual investments which yield gener-

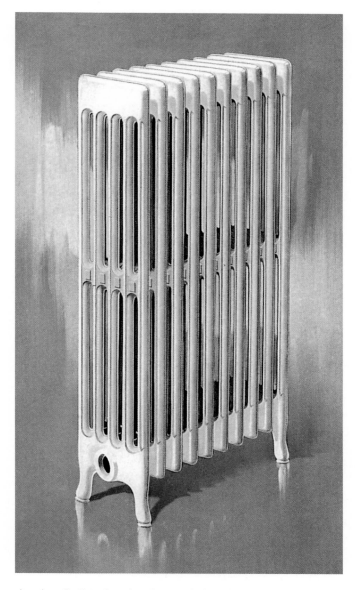

American Radiator introduced a new design, the "Corto," in 1917, to satisfy the need for grace and utility.

ous dividends, while adding greater value to the buildings in which they are installed. In a few years they pay for themselves in the fuel they save," noted the 1921 Annual Report.

Clarence Woolley established the Institute of Thermal Research during the war to help find new, more efficient heaters to run on fuels other than precious (and scarce) coal and oil. The Ideal Arcola Radiator Boiler brought a new design at a

THE RADIATOR BUILDING

AMERICAN RADIATOR PROSPERED LIKE many companies in the booming economy following World War I. In 1922, Clarence Woolley commissioned noted architect Raymond Hood to design an impressive headquarters building befitting the corporation's standing in the industry. The 21-story building that rose at 40 West 40th Street in Manhattan was a brooding black neo-Gothic tower with a gold-leaf crown. Considered a striking example of modern architecture when completed, the building was said to resemble a radiator, its golden crown symbolizing radiant heat, especially when viewed at night.

Hood "rocketed to prominence in 1922 when he won the international competition for *The Chicago Tribune's* new office tower," wrote a *New York Times* reporter. "Hood embraced both the aesthetic and the business sides of architecture. ... The building opened in 1924 and embodied several departures from existing practice."[1]

Woolley and Hood "both had ideas about the blackness of buildings," *Fortune* magazine reported in 1935. Overseas during World War I, "Mr. Woolley had seen old and blackened structures abroad and had found them very picturesque and

time when conservation was critical. The hot-water-heating boiler burned natural or artificial gas and provided hot water for both daily living and heating radiators.

The Arcola Radiator Boiler and an accompanying package of vent fittings brought heat to every room. One customer wrote that "we have always heated our house with stoves and have experienced the discomfort of having one room hot and the others cold for more than 27 years. With Arcola, we have, for the first time, the satisfaction of enjoying every room in our home."[24]

By 1924, profits had topped $10 million, and Woolley decided it was time to erect a corporate headquarters building as a testimonial to the company's success. He commissioned architect Raymond Hood to design the "black tower" that was completed in 1924 at 40 West 40th Street. Reminiscent of the office towers Woolley had seen and admired in Europe, the slender black building with gold spires faced Bryant Park in Manhattan. (It was recognized as a historic building in 1962.)

effective, while Mr. Hood had a theory that most skyscrapers looked as though they were shot full of holes (windows). Whereas the proper effect of substance and solidity could be had by making the walls dark as well as the windows."[2]

Though newer, taller buildings sprung up around it, the "Radiator Building" endured as an important landmark. "The building rises a mere 21 stories but because of its sleek verticals can actually be seen to soar," *New York Magazine* noted in 1983. "The black brick of the skin was chosen to emphasize the mass of what is in fact a very slender building, and the gold of the spiky Gothic filials was intended to bestow a radiance appropriate to the owner's products."[3]

In honor of the building's 50th anniversary, a restoration of the black gothic tower with its signature gold spires got underway in 1974. "While this will require a great deal of work," said Harry Gilmore, manager of corporate facilities, "the job is mainly a cosmetic one because the building's facade has been kept exactly as the architect designed it."[4]

Workmen removed corrosion from the bronze doors and trim on the building. Marble was also replaced in the bulkheads supporting the windows. When the building was first erected, people thought the black color with gold trim was chosen to represent coal and the energy given off by burning fuel. Hood set the record straight.

"Chairman Woolley and I had each been impressed by the magnificence of gold ornamentation on old buildings black with age in London and Brussels. On a tall building in New York City, the result could be gloomy and depressing, but I knew management to be tolerant men appreciative of the difficulties of design and of doing a new thing for which there was little, if any, precedent."[5]

As *New York Magazine* noted, "the Radiator Building, with its ebullient ornament draping a serenely confident form, is an enduring reminder of the essence of the skyscraper when it was young."[6]

Although the company's growth would slow during the Great Depression, the tower remained as a monument to the golden age of the radiator. "Mr. Woolley's tower is famous — that neo-Gothic shaft of funereal black brick, relieved by a gold crown," *Fortune* magazine would note in the depths of the Depression, comparing this edifice to Woolley himself.

"The U.S. building industry is currently moribund and the American Radiator Building, which is representative of that industry, is a pile of dead black bricks ... but the building has a crown of gold leaf and Chairman Woolley is an indefatigable optimist who talks of greater booms than we have ever known."[25]

In 1928, the year before Woolley would orchestrate the second big merger in the company's history, he told a group of college graduates at a June commencement, "You will succeed best where interest ascends unto a genuine love for the job."

By 1929, American Radiator had subsidiaries in nine European countries and had become the world leader in heating products. Woolley kept up the practice of acquiring companies to cement American Radiator's leadership. He had engineered the purchase in 1922 of the Detroit Lubricator Company, a producer of locomotive lubricators and automobile carburetors, as well as a line of radiator valves, air valves, thermostats and other heating accessories sold under the name "Genuine Detroit."[26]

But Woolley recognized that even greater opportunity existed in the market for construction supplies, and he turned his attention to creating a mega-merger, which would result in a union with Standard Sanitary Manufacturing Company.

"The Plumber Protects the Health of the Nation," a portrait of the Master Plumber hanging in American Standard's headquarters.

CHAPTER TWO

THE RISE OF STANDARD SANITARY

1875–1929

"His mission one of Cleanliness! To teach
The open road of Life's supernal wealth
To guide and aid his fellowman to reach
The treasure trove that lies in perfect health."

— Theodore Ahrens: A Tribute, date unknown[1]

THE HISTORY OF STANDARD Sanitary Manufacturing Company mirrors that of American Radiator. Both became public companies in 1899. In each case, entrepreneurs with foresight recognized potential in products that relied on newly developed material; both companies rose to dominate their respective industries; both essentially served the same customers; both were born from the merger of other companies.

Standard Sanitary emerged in 1899 principally from the union of Ahrens & Ott Manufacturing of Louisville, Kentucky; Standard Manufacturing of Pittsburgh, Pennsylvania; and Dawes & Myler Manufacturing, founded by two men from Standard Manufacturing. Six smaller firms (Buick and Sherwood, Volrath, Pennsylvania Bath, Cribben, Sanitary Manufacturing and Enameling and Victor) were also absorbed.

Led by Theodore Ahrens, Standard Sanitary quickly dominated the enameled cast-iron plumbing industry by staying out in front with new developments and processes.

A Brief History of Sanitation

No other single factor in the history of public health is as important as the advancement of sanitation. Most of the epidemics and plagues that historically decimated populations had their roots in the improper disposal of waste and the lack of per-

sonal hygiene. Public health historian John Duffy, author of *The Sanitarians, A History of Sanitation in America*, wrote that "the history of public health shows that cities tend to grow faster than the ability of municipal officials to cope with health and sanitary matters."[2]

As villages formed into towns and cities, the problem of waste disposal grew. In the Middle Ages, crowded conditions worsened as people dumped human waste and garbage unceremoniously into the streets for the rats to devour. With the rats came fleas, and with the fleas came the bubonic plague, the "Black Death." The plague reached Europe in 1348, and by 1351 the disease had wiped out an estimated 25 million people — roughly one-third of the population of Europe.[3]

The Black Death and more common epidemics (a grim menu that included cholera, typhoid fever, yellow fever and dysentery) gradually forced public officials to enact sanitary measures. In the United States, these changes occurred slowly. Sanitary methods remained basically unchanged until the late 1800s, and severe outbreaks of cholera hit the entire eastern part of the United States several times during that century. New Orleans, for example, was devastated in 1832 by cholera, caused by

A "washstand" from the 1885 catalog.

a fecal-borne bacteria that infects food and water. About 15,000 people out of a population of 50,000 fled the city; of the remaining 35,000 residents, between 4,500 and 5,000 died of the disease.[4]

In the 1880s, the United States experienced a revolution in sanitation as scientific discovery unlocked the nature of disease. Cholera, for example, almost disappeared following German bacteriologist Robert Koch's 1883 discovery that bacteria from improperly disposed fecal matter posed a public health threat.[5] This breakthrough in microbiology spurred the growth of sewer lines, a utility that had obvious advantages as far back as Roman times. But sewer systems are expensive to install and maintain, and many municipalities were reluctant to invest in such a venture until the health benefits were made obvious.

The toilet, on the other hand, enjoyed rapid improvements since its introduction. Popular legend credits the invention of the toilet to Englishman Thomas Crapper, but Crapper had little to do with the advent of the water closet (later known as the toilet). *Plumbing & Mechanical Magazine* conducted interviews with scholars who had researched Thomas Crapper's life, and found no evidence that Crapper invented the toilet,

although he did win patents on devices to improve drains and plumbing, as well as operate plumbing shops. Contrary to legend, Thomas Crapper was never knighted (and thus should not be known as Sir Thomas Crapper), although he did serve as the royal sanitary engineer for members of the Crown.[6] It took the inventive genius of many people over hundreds of years to perfect the commode.

Building upon their work, Americans Charles Neff and Robert Frame introduced in the early 1900s a siphonic washdown closet, an innovation that would become the standard in the United States.[7] The siphonic washdown closet used several water pipes and a jet action to clean the rim and basin and provide a cleansing after-flush of water. An ample water supply with proper pressure made this advance possible as the principles of mass production made public sewer and water systems possible. By 1910, American cities had more than 25,000 miles of sewer lines, greatly reducing the outbreak of epidemics.

Arrott and Torrance

Two Irish immigrants, James Arrott and Francis J. Torrance, grasped that sanitation, indoor

1875 — Ahrens & Ott Manufacturing is founded.

1879 — Two former Standard Manufacturing employees start up Dawes & Myler Manufacturing.

1875

1875 — James Arrott and Francis Torrance found Standard Manufacturing Company.

bathrooms and plumbing were growth industries. In 1875, the partners bought a bankrupt kitchen-ware factory in Pittsburgh, Pennsylvania, and began making cast-iron water closets, washstands and bathtubs. They named their new company Standard Manufacturing.

Bathtubs had evolved slowly from Benjamin Franklin's boot-shaped model, but most had been made of wood, lined with copper, galvanized iron or zinc, and painted white. Some affluent home-owners had tubs that could be folded into spe-cially designed cabinets that matched the furni-ture in their bedrooms.[8] Later designs featured sheet metal with wooden rims, but the tubs were again available only in painted white. Early bath-tubs were heavy, between 450 and 500 pounds, and expensive. In 1883, Standard Manufacturing perfected a new process to coat pulverized enam-el onto hot castings to form a smooth, white sur-face that was easy to clean. An 1890 catalog described the manufacturing process.

"Perchance this pamphlet may fall into the hands of one who does not fully know what a porcelain enameled bath tub is. ... To begin with, the tub is cast in iron, made of the best quality pig metal. After

This very modest damsel of the 15th century took her bath in this tub shaped like a shoe. Once she was inside, only her neck and head emerged. Thus she could receive callers while in her bath if she wished.

1899 — Following a wave of merg-ers, Standard Sanitary Manufacturing Corporation emerges, with Theodore Ahrens as president.

1929

1885 — Theodore Ahrens buys into his father's business and becomes general manager.

1929 — Standard Sanitary launches a new concept: make a bathroom an aesthetically integral part of the home.

publish a lavishly illustrated *Color and Style in Bathroom Furnishings and Decoration* that provided not only color schemes, but suggestions on the layout for a bathroom. Its stated purpose was to aesthetically integrate the bathroom into the home.

Color and Style in Bathroom Furnishings and Decoration

STANDARD SANITARY BROKE with tradition in 1929 when it demonstrated how the bathroom could be both utilitarian and beautiful. Until then, the bathroom was largely considered a "necessary room," or an indoor outhouse. Advances in lithography enabled the company to

being cast in a sand mold, it is thoroughly cleaned by 'pickling,' a process which removes all sand, scale and other foreign substances and leaves a surface of smooth, clean iron.

"It is then coated thinly with porcelain in solution and dried gradually, leaving a white precipitate on the surface of the iron. The casting of the tub is then subjected to intense heat ... and the porcelain and iron are fused together making a thorough amalgamation of the two substances. While the tub is still at a bright red heat, the porcelain enamel is applied in a powdered form as fine as flour, which readily adheres to the heated surface and is there to stay."[9]

The men launched a campaign to persuade consumers of the porcelain enameled cast-iron bathtub's sanitary advantages, but its high cost made it difficult for people to afford. A basic 6-foot painted tub cost $26 while a porcelain enameled tub of the same size could be had for $50. Bathtubs could also be purchased in four lengths ranging from 4 feet to $5\frac{1}{2}$ feet. Among the most expensive in the 1890 catalog was the "Royal Albion Bath" with an exterior of polished cast bronze depicting cherubs and a porcelain enameled interior. This 5-foot tub cost $250.

A porcelain enameled product was clearly superior because it enhanced beauty and, more importantly, made a product virtually impervious to water. Metal or wood tubs and basins invariably

corroded as bacteria multiplied on the sides and in nooks and crannies. Porcelain enameling provided a durable coating that did not absorb water. Porcelain was first developed by the Chinese in the 6th century A.D. and had been imported into Europe for centuries. It wasn't until the early 1700s that Europe made its own high-quality porcelain products, but they were mainly used in art. Technology gradually improved, but it was not possible to porcelainize everyday products until Standard Sanitary found a way to spread the material evenly, without cracking.

"Almost immediately, they began a spirited drive to convert people from the old sheet-metal tub with its unsanitary rim to the cleaner and sightlier enameled one," according to a brief history of American Radiator & Standard Sanitary Corporation.

"Without pause, from that day to this, Standard Manufacturing Company and its successor companies have aggressively promoted better sanitation and better plumbing fixtures. Their unceasing efforts have accomplished much in raising the standards of living throughout the world and have contributed largely to the growth of the plumbing industry and the success of our present company."[10]

The porcelain enameled tubs varied in price because the trimmings and exterior finish varied in detail; the quality of

Above right: This fine "Royal Albion Bath" sold for $250 enameled.

Below: The more pedestrian "Albion" patterned enameled bathtub sold for $50.

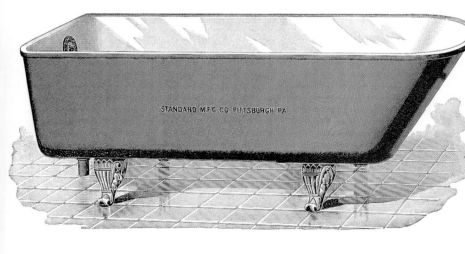

the enamel was the same on all tubs, according to a brochure. "Until lately, it has been the custom to 'hide' everything in the shape of a bath tub because it was unsightly. Through this company's efforts a bath tub has been produced that will vie with any piece of household furnishment in point of finish and attractiveness."[11] (During this period the bathtub was typically spelled as two words.)

Two Standard Manufacturing employees, Edward L. Dawes and William A. Myler, had left the company in 1879 to start a factory under their own names. The factory was located in New Brighton, Pennsylvania, and manufactured cast-iron enameled bathtubs. But as their business grew, they expanded into enameled bathroom-related products such as sinks and toilets.

Ahrens & Ott

Meanwhile, in Louisville, Kentucky, another company was entering the enamelware market. Ahrens & Ott Manufacturing of Louisville, Kentucky, had started out in 1860 as a brass foundry but by 1894 had become one of the leading makers of the popular enameled, cast-iron bathtubs, sinks and bathroom fixtures. The company was founded by Theodore Ahrens (the father of Standard Sanitary's Theodore Ahrens, nicknamed "Thee" by his parents) and Henry L. Ott.

"Thee" Ahrens was born in Baltimore in 1859, the son of parents who had emigrated from Germany five years earlier. Following Thee's birth, the family moved to Louisville, Kentucky, where the elder Ahrens founded the business with plumber Henry Ott. It was Ott who first suggested that the foundry expand into plumbing products.

At 13, Thee Ahrens began working part-time at the foundry with his father. He quickly

learned the art of brass molding and finishing, a trade that would remain important to him throughout his career. Just as he was preparing to enter high school, his father broke the news that Thee was needed full-time in the foundry, ending the boy's education.

Ahrens may have lacked a formal education, but a later biography would note that his "university has been the school of experience, and his teachers have been his fellow men, men from all walks of life, but more particularly, leaders of thought and action in the building industry."[12]

From his father, Ahrens learned to "stick to the job and do your duty, no matter how unpleasant."[13] He shouldered heavy responsibilities, including maintaining the fire under the foundry boiler. His father's lesson was driven home one day when he left the boiler to play baseball in a field next to the foundry. The water level dropped below the danger line. Ahrens returned to find his father furiously raking a fire from under the boiler, which was about to explode. The older man screamed to his son to run and save his own life, but Ahrens stayed, helped his father put out the fire and saved the boiler.

He credited his later success to his mother, Christine Marie Lohman Ahrens.

"It is to the wise counsel, help and encouragement given by my mother — to her broad and generous spirit, to her splendid character — that I owe a large part of whatever I have accomplished. She was a large-hearted and kind influence for her children."[14]

Ahrens' relationship with his father appears to have been more complex. The younger Ahrens left the foundry over a salary dispute when he was 19. During the six years he had worked there, his salary had risen from $2.50 to $7.50 per week. Denied a raise by his father, Ahrens left home and worked in larger brass foundries in Massachusetts and New York City

Theodore Ahrens had left home at 19 to learn all he could about plumbing. He returned in 1885 and built a worldwide plumbing powerhouse.

to "learn all there was to know about the plumbing business."[15]

Ahrens returned to Louisville a few years later and bought into his father's business in 1885.[16] Becoming a stockholder, Ahrens became treasurer and general manager. Ahrens' father and Henry Ott had wanted him to work on straight salary, but the young man insisted that he and his brothers and colleagues receive company stock, arguing that it would build a feeling of ownership among them.

The principle of ownership was one he would follow as the business expanded and the company began hiring employees who were not family members. "Taking these men in as stockholders was really the first step we made toward stock ownership by employees," he later remarked. "It established the principle and proved the value of it. Year after year we saw how a common interest was of mutual advantage — to the individual and to the company, finally resulting in the great organization we have now."[17]

The Merger

By 1898, Ahrens and Ott, Standard Sanitary and Dawes and Myler had become leaders in the enamel- and sanitary-ware industries. The companies followed the wave of consolidations that swept across many industries during this period. A contemporary journalist observed the rise of the corporation and the demise of the single proprietor.

"Throughout America, during the latter half of the 19th century, continued a process of little shops closing down, big factories growing bigger; little one-man businesses giving up, great corporations growing and expanding; rural communities becoming stagnant, big cities pulsing forward; farm districts thinning out, cities growing denser."[18]

National advertising had elevated the name of Standard Manufacturing to prominence in the trade and the general public.

When the companies merged, the officers decided to keep "Standard" in the new name. The new partners wisely chose Ahrens to lead their new Pittsburgh-based Standard Sanitary Manufacturing Company, capitalized at $4 million. A master plumber, Ahrens was also a consummate salesman, and for the next 30 years, Standard Sanitary dominated the plumbing supply business.

Ahrens, a plumber first and foremost, had earned the respect of plumbers worldwide. Before the heyday of direct-to-customer retailers such as Sears, Roebuck, master plumbers handled the installation of plumbing fixtures, so this relationship was crucial to Standard Sanitary. Sales were made to wholesale outlets, which increased as Standard Sanitary acquired smaller firms such as Northwestern Pipe & Supply Company of Erie, Pennsylvania (1906); Pittsburgh Supply Company of Pittsburgh (1911); Higgins Company of San Antonio, Texas (1913); Republic Manufacturing Company of Chicago, Illinois (1914); and the L.M. Rumsey Company of St. Louis, Missouri (1917).

Cornering the Market

From the beginning, Standard Sanitary set out to produce a one-piece bathtub. By 1900, it

The legs and artistic side pieces of this Standard Manufacturing tub were cast from solid bronze, and topped by a walnut rim.

had succeeded. Within a year of the merger, Standard was producing 150 tubs per day and had become the largest supplier of plumbing goods in the world. Continuing research yielded important developments: Arrott developed a mechanically vibrating sieve that cut enameling time in half. John C. Reed, the Allegheny plant superintendent, developed an even faster process for mechanically enameling tubs, toilets and sinks. He patented the process, known as the match-plate system or the Reed Method. Previously, the sieve process had been done by hand. Both improvements made it possible for the company to manufacture the first one-piece all-over enameled tub.

In 1904, the company expanded its advertising and education campaign to include showrooms to allow consumers to see the products for themselves. In 1913, Standard Sanitary purchased the Great Western Pottery Company of Ohio and began manufacturing porcelain enamelware.[19] Three years later the company introduced a complete line of cast-iron enameled kitchen sinks. The sinks did not fare well until the company featured them at the Pittsburgh Annual Exposition.

The advantages were slow to catch on, in spite of the improvements in cleaning and general sanitation. Ahrens noted that older consumers were hard to convince.

"These farmers and small town homeowners are being educated through their children in the schools and the advertising in their papers and magazines that plumbing to be healthful must be safe, to be safe must be done by men skilled in its application."[20]

But it did eventually replace the old painted tub. The revolution in sanitation was in full swing in the early 1900s as more cities devoted resources to public sewage, and the bathroom continued to

John C. Reed, superintendent of the Allegheny plant, developed a process he patented to enamel tubs quickly; he also fathered a future president of American Radiator & Standard Sanitary.

move indoors. The master plumber was placed on his pedestal; the company warned the public that the plumber's contribution to the health and welfare of the household was not to be taken lightly. Standard Sanitary cautioned consumers to "choose your plumber as you would your physician. You should be on intimate terms with your chosen plumber since he is the physician who will cure the ills of your sewage, gas and water systems."

Advertisements during this period reinforced the message: "Both heating and plumbing are too essential to the welfare of your family and to the uninterrupted enjoyment of your home to be entrusted to any but the skilled hands of a Heating and Plumbing contractor" and "Only the Master Plumbers have the knowledge, experience, and skill necessary to protect the health of the nation by correct installation."[21]

During the next 25 years, Standard would produce close to 7 million bathtubs. By 1925 the company would be worth $40 million and employ 9,250. Standard Sanitary's first plant occupied just two-thirds of an acre, but by 1925, its combined factories occupied 2.5 million square feet spread over 50 acres. The company then had six domestic factories, one Canadian factory, 15 British sales offices, 34 branch houses, 36 showrooms and six warehouses. In 1927, the company established a factory in Neuss, Germany.

The Bathroom Comes of Age

White had been the standard color in homes because it was easy to clean and gave an impression of being sanitary. But in 1926, the year acid-resisting enamel was introduced, color made its appearance.

The introduction of color opened a new chapter in the history of the bathroom. In 1929, the company published a booklet titled *Color and Style in Bathroom Furnishings and Decoration.* In this groundbreaking publication, Standard Sanitary acknowledged that it took a "new and different attitude" toward the bathroom in relation to the household:

"That attitude may be summed up in the question: 'Why shouldn't the bathroom be given as much consideration as an interior as other rooms in the home?' This question was an outlet from the anchorage of tradition. It was an embarkation point for a voyage in which the only guidance was charted in the principles that function determines form, that the practical can and should be beautiful."[22]

The booklet waging the new campaign first considered the function of the bathroom and how to expand its usefulness. Colors were examined to provide the reader with ideas for choosing the bathroom's layout and the size and placement of windows and fixtures, along with a detailed color scheme. The brochure's writer mused on the fact that Standard Sanitary had no precedent to guide it:

"The bathroom is a development of the past 25 years, and that development waited upon the development of sewerage systems. ... Originality in bathroom architecture has been stultified by the casual and undistinguished beginning of the room itself. Its importance as a factor in health and comfort was accepted generally. With its utility solely in mind, the home owner decided to install a bathroom in his home; so he converted another room, a large closet, or a hall into a bathroom. And this ignoble beginning has left its mark upon the bathroom of today. ...

"Just as beauty in the living room cannot be disassociated from the design of the furniture, so the beauty of the bathroom must have its beginning in the design of the plumbing fixtures. ... Function determines form. But within the limits set by function must be found the way to beauty of design. 'Standard' designers found that way."[23]

With the acceptance of the bathroom as an integral and attractive part of the house, Standard Sanitary continued its rapid growth. By the time Clarence Woolley approached Ahrens to discuss his plans for a mega-merger, Standard Sanitary, the world's largest producer of plumbing supplies, employed more than 12,000 and turned out thousands of fixtures a day.

In this 1925 advertisement, a master plumber is shown explaining to a child the importance of using the right products to protect his health.

The Tonawanda Iron Corporation had been acquired by American Radiator in 1923. It became a subsidiary of American Radiator & Standard Sanitary Corporation in 1929.

CHAPTER THREE

JOINING FORCES—AR&SS SURVIVES THE DEPRESSION

1929–1939

"Every time you turn on the heat or draw yourself a glass of water or flush a toilet, the chances are just about fifty-fifty that you are dealing with Mr. Woolley's machinery."

— *Fortune* magazine, 1935[1]

BY 1929, STANDARD SANITARY Manufacturing Corporation and American Radiator Company had become giants in their respective industries, their products installed in nearly half of the dwellings in the United States and Europe. A merger between the two seemed logical for a number of reasons: Both companies used pig iron as their raw material, both were major producers of cast iron and both worked closely with the construction industry. At the time, building products were bought and installed by craftsmen. Merged, the company could offer contractors one-stop shopping and perpetuate its lock on the construction products market.

The union occurred after American Radiator's Clarence Woolley tried to engineer an ambitious but doomed mega-merger with Standard Sanitary, Johns-Manville (the biggest American manufacturer of synthetic housing materials) and Otis Elevator Company (the biggest U.S. elevator manufacturer) into an immense powerhouse. A unified sales force would have offered contractors virtually everything they needed from one company. Business analysts believed that America was on the cusp of a major building boom, so prosperity for the new conglomerate seemed assured.

"But terms were never reached; the merger never happened," *Fortune* noted. "What did happen, however, was ambitious enough."[2] The nego-

tiations broke down with Otis and Johns-Manville, so Woolley turned his attention to Standard Sanitary because Ahrens was still very much interested. Woolley and Ahrens began organizing the American Radiator-Standard Sanitary merger in early 1928 and pulled the transaction together by year's end.[3]

The deal consummated, Woolley sent a message to shareholders in American Radiator's 37th Annual Report, released December 31, 1928.

"Notices have been sent to all shareholders of your Company giving full particulars respecting a union of interests of American Radiator Company and Standard Sanitary Manufacturing. These companies entered upon their careers as public companies in the same year — 1899. Their growth has been parallel respecting volume and profits in the United States. The marketing of products through the same customers, with warehouses and selling branches in the same important industrial centers, presents an opportunity for these different but related industries substantial-

---

With the slogan "The Best Seat in the House," the Church Company became a subsidiary of the new holding company, American Radiator & Standard Sanitary Corporation, in 1929.

ly to enlarge their aggregate volume of business. It is hoped that American Radiator & Standard Sanitary Corporation, the new holding company, will be in active operation on or about April 1, 1929, or sooner, if meanwhile two-thirds of the stock of each company is placed with the depositories provided for that purpose."[4]

On March 26, 1929, the American Radiator & Standard Sanitary Corporation became a legal entity under the laws of the state of Delaware. The merged company had combined assets of $187.6 million, and its future looked bright. Woolley became chairman of the board of the new holding company; Ahrens, president; Charles H. Hodges, vice president; and R.J. Hamilton, secretary and treasurer. The following year, Hamilton was elected president and secretary of American Radiator; Henry M. Reed (son of Allegheny plant Superintendent John Reed) was elected president and chairman of the executive committee of Standard Sanitary. In 1929, 47,000 shares of preferred stock and about 10 million shares of common stock were issued.

Manowitch Brothers, New York City investment analysts, published an optimistic report of the merger in May 1929.

"Closely related to construction activity, they have shared in its prosperity developing a larger earning power, broadening the scope of operations, and building up financial strength. ... The merger of American Radiator Company and Standard Sanitary Manufacturing Company into American Radiator & Standard Sanitary Corporation is expected to facilitate sales stimulation, real economies, and expansion possibilities which add materially to earnings and to the intrinsic values of the securities of the new Corporation."[5]

But from the start, the company was unified in name only. "They got together in 1929 — and for 10 years they pursued their depressing courses realizing only a small fraction of the savings or other advantages that had been advanced as reasons for their union," one *Fortune* magazine article noted in 1939. "If anything, they got into each other's way."[6]

American Radiator & Standard Sanitary Corporation functioned as a holding company for American Radiator, Standard Sanitary Manufacturing Company and about 18 subsidiaries. Each operated under its own name and management.[7] The divisions functioned

March 1929 — American Radiator and Standard Sanitary merge.

1932 — American Radiator & Standard Sanitary posts a $6 million loss during the Depression's darkest year.

1929

October 1929 — Stock market crash heralds the Great Depression.

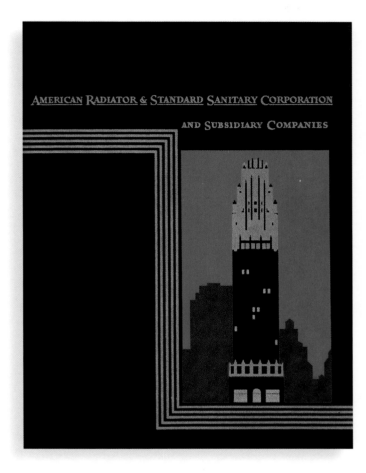

AMERICAN RADIATOR & STANDARD SANITARY CORPORATION

AND SUBSIDIARY COMPANIES

autonomously, and with friction whenever their paths crossed.

Whether the divisions of American Radiator & Standard Sanitary Corporation got along or not, AR&SS's fortune depended upon a healthy construction industry. From that point of view, its market potential looked unlimited. At the time of the merger, an increasing population drove a sustained building boom. Manowitch Brothers analyst Bernard Henick estimated that the building industry was kept busy with roughly $5 billion (in 1929 dollars) in new construction. Each year of the previous four years was better than the last. "In other words, the building industry is not subjected to radical variations of yearly expansion and depression, rather its activity proceeds at a regular, normal annual rate."[8] That was about to change.

By 1931, AR&SS had 40 American and European affiliated companies. Merging the plumbing and heating giants, and their respective subsidiaries, under a holding company required a directory for product lines and the companies that produced them.

1934 — Theodore Ahrens retires as president of the corporation; Clarence Woolley assumes responsibilities.

1938 — Henry Reed becomes president following a challenge to Woolley's leadership.

1939

1936 — Changes in the tax law prompt Woolley to consider dissolving the holding company in favor of a merged operating company.

The Great Depression

Few people recognized that the American economy teetered on overvalued stock speculation and mass consumer debt. When boom turned to bust seven months later, the belief in the age of permanent prosperity evaporated.

Stock prices began their precipitous slide on October 18, 1929. The first day of real panic, October 24, blue chip certificates of companies like General Electric, Johns-Manville and Montgomery Ward tumbled, in some cases losing 25 percent of their value.

On October 29, "Black Tuesday," frantic investors, bankers and investment companies unloaded 16 million shares of stock, heralding the start of the Great Depression, which would consume the livelihoods, dreams and dignity of millions of American workers and families. At the depth of the Depression, 16 million Americans — a quarter of the working-age population — would be out of work. Those lucky enough to have savings accounts raided them. In 1932 alone, 3,646 banks closed down.

President Herbert Hoover insisted that "prosperity is just around the corner," but the millions of people forced to live in dilapidated wooden shacks, which they dubbed "Hoovervilles," gave lie to that claim. Housing starts had begun to fall off even before the crash. "During the months of January, February and March 1929, building activity began to decline, especially in residential construction, the class from which American Radiator Company and Standard Sanitary Mfg. Company derive their largest patronage," Woolley wrote in the 1929 Annual Report, the first issued for the combined companies. "During each month thereafter the percentage of decline was greater and by the first of August had reached very great proportions."[9] In the last quarter of 1929, contracts for new residential buildings "fell off 40 percent to 50 percent."[10]

That year, net profits were $20 million, down about 4.8 percent from the previous year's $21 million.[11] Sales in Europe remained strong, with profits and business volume abroad actually increasing. Throughout much of the Great Depression that followed, foreign sales would help keep the domestic operation afloat. National Radiator Company, Limited, the English subsidiary, changed its name to Ideal Boilers & Radiators, Limited, late in the decade because its Ideal products enjoyed wide popularity in England.[12]

Also in 1929, the holding company made its first acquisition when it purchased the Church Company, a toilet seat manufacturer in Holyoke, Massachusetts. For 56,000 shares of American Radiator & Standard Sanitary stock and assumption of outstanding notes, the company acquired Church and its slogan, "The Best Seat in the House."[13] The company operated as a wholly owned subsidiary.

The Church Company began when its founder, Charles F. Church, invented a method for coating brass bed parts with white pyroxylin. The new process made the brass beds more durable and, he hoped, more attractive. Consumers didn't agree, and the company faltered. In 1906, the business was sold, and the new owners decided to apply the process to

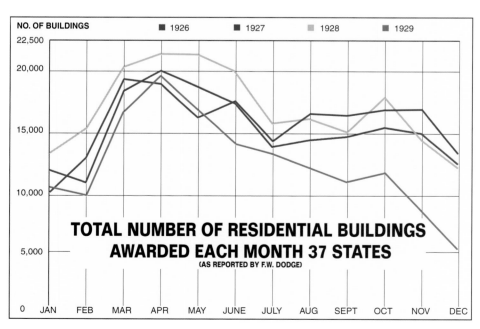

By the end of the Roaring '20s, it was clear the building boom was over for awhile.

toilet seats, made of oak or mahogany. The "Church seat" was a success. By 1929, when American Radiator & Standard Sanitary purchased the company, sales had reached $2 million and the toilet seat manufacturer employed 175.[14]

By the beginning of the 1930s, the crash was making its effects felt and the downturn in the building industry continued. Profits for 1930 had shrunk to $6.6 million. Just one year later, profits plummeted to just $200,646.[15]

A Lonely Voice of Optimism

Woolley insisted better times were ahead. Young couples had put marriage plans on hold and many families had moved in together to save money, so Woolley predicted that pent-up demand would explode as soon as the economy improved.[16] But in the dark days of the early thirties, there seemed no end to the Depression. In 1932, the nation's bleakest year, American Radiator & Standard Sanitary Corporation produced a net loss of nearly $6 million, and the company laid off more than a thousand workers.

In spite of Woolley's lonely claim of better times ahead, his annual letter to shareholders reflected the national gloom:

"The severity of the current business depression has affected the building industry in greater measure than during any period in the history of the major component units of your Company. Contracts for residential floor space awarded in 1932 declined to the lowest levels of the current century and were 87 percent below those of the year 1928."[17]

Franklin Delano Roosevelt, elected in 1932, quickly moved to institute his "New Deal" reforms. He persuaded Congress to create the Federal Deposit Insurance Corporation to guarantee bank deposits, establish a Home Owners Loan Corporation to facilitate mortgage lending, and fund the Civilian Conservation Corps to reduce unemployment. The federal government spent more than $500 million during Roosevelt's first term to get the country back on track, but its efforts were only a partial cure.[18] Testifying before the Senate Banking Committee in 1932, Woolley supported

C. F. CHURCH MANUFACTURING COMPANY

CHURCH SANI-BLACK SEATS

CHURCH SANI-BLACK SEATS are a composition hard rubber product, created for public buildings where unusual abuse may be expected. They are produced through the combined processes of hydraulic pressure and veneering.

The surface is thick composition hard rubber, vulcanized in a mold under 216,000 lbs. of hydraulic heat pressure. This produces a hard, smooth, indestructible finish.

The Core consists of a solid, compact unit made entirely from hydraulic pressed wood fibres. The fibres are in their natural wood state, thereby retaining the lignins (nature's resinous cohesive binder). The core thus formed has all the elements of natural wood, plus the advantage of having no grain or cross grain. This is a distinct advantage in a toilet seat as it removes the possibility of cracking or splitting. The core is laminated, 3 ply.

In combining the core and rubber covering we have produced a seat that has no joints or seams; a seat where both core and covering are of uniform resiliency, shock absorbent, flexible to contortion, tough, hygienic and indestructible.

Church Sani-Black Seats are acid resisting, moisture proof, and attractive in appearance.

Important Feature
An important hinge feature of CHURCH Sani-Black seats is the solid steel insert which is molded into the core under 108 ton hydraulic pressure. The hinge is attached to the seat by means of heavy machine screws which are gripped by these threaded inserts, as shown, making it impossible for the hinge to loosen or the screws to pull out.

NOTE CONCEALED SOLID STEEL INSERT MOLDED INTO SEAT

Guarantee
The C.F. Church Mfg. Co. guarantees CHURCH SANI-BLACK Seats and Covers and will furnish new seats and covers free of charge, in exchange for any that might break, split, crack, chip, scale or craze.
C.F. CHURCH MFG. CO.

[The value of a guarantee can be measured only by the honesty and integrity of the concern making the guarantee]

Many of the companies purchased by AR&SS had their own rich histories. The Church Company, for example, had been making toilet seats for such august structures as the New Yorker Hotel since 1906.

government intervention. "I think we are mighty near the turning point," he said, "and with a little help from you gentlemen, business can get on its feet very quickly."[19]

By 1933, Woolley believed the worst had passed. At the company's April 12, 1933, annual meeting, when he reported the previous year's loss to shareholders, he noted: "We have passed through this ordeal with rather good results, notwithstanding that we have suffered a loss. ... We may be right now at the crossroads."[20]

Building activity increased slightly that year, and the company was able to put more people to work. In May of that year, Standard's Louisville

FROM THE GRIDIRON TO THE BOARDROOM

HENRY REED FORCED A SHOWDOWN with Clarence Woolley over the direction of American Radiator & Standard Sanitary Corporation and would become chairman of a new, leaner company. But he was originally hired for a far different reason: his skill at football.

Courted by colleges upon his high school graduation in 1897, Reed, the son of Allegheny plant Superintendent John C. Reed, achieved national recognition playing for the Western University of Pennsylvania, which would later become the University of Pittsburgh.

Shortly after winning his varsity letter, he was approached by a representative of Standard Sanitary, who offered him the opportunity to make money at the sport. As a publicity scheme, Standard Sanitary had organized a company football team and wanted to recruit talent. Reed joined as a ringer and, when the football season was over, went on to prove his talents off the field.[1]

Reed was born in Millvale, Pennsylvania (a Pittsburgh suburb), on September 16, 1880, one of seven children. His father had developed the patented "Reed Method" for mechanically enameling tubs, toilets and lavatories.

Henry Reed played football for Standard Sanitary and worked there part time while he finished college. In 1902, Reed joined the company as an enamel mixer, entrusted with the secret formulas for compounding, melting and milling enamels. He rose swiftly to become the superintendent of the enamel mixing department, and in 1907 he became an assistant man-

ager of the Standard Works. Three years later he became manager of the Louisville Works — the company's largest manufacturing unit. From 1913 to 1924 Reed was assistant general manager of factories and was elected to the board of directors. He became general manager of factories in 1924 (as vice president), and that same year he was appointed to the executive committee. In 1928 he was named first vice president and chairman of the executive committee. After the 1929 merger he became president of Standard Sanitary, and in 1938 he became chairman of the board and president of the new company.

There was never any question about Reed's common sense management style. Upon his retirement, Bill Stern, a commentator for NBC, summed it up.

"He is a natural empiricist. Harboring an almost congenital aversion for theories and pure research, he is inclined to rely upon naked judgment or conditioned hunches. This apparently is an ingenuous aspect of his sincere dislike for artifice and ostentation, which supplements his habit of avoiding public affairs and minding his own business. He is not bashful, and instantly can distinguish first-rate from second-rate rye, though he is not allowed to do so at home, where he is the essence of philoprogeneity. He acts and talks with a profane, blustery forthrightness that connotes a lifelong association with the somewhat belligerent manliness of the bathtub foundry."[2]

plant brought back 1,200 men, increasing its workforce to a pre-Depression level of 3,528.[21] Still, between 1933 and 1935 the company eliminated common stock dividends.

In 1934, American Radiator & Standard Sanitary entered the air conditioning business. Woolley recognized the promise of air conditioning, though the technology was still being developed. The company wanted to bring the infant air conditioning industry "out of the gadget stage," said Fowler Manning, head of the new Standard Air Conditioning Division.

"Inasmuch as air conditioning is an extension of heating and ventilating, our first resolution is that heating and the heating trade shall be the beneficiaries of this new market. ... [The company] is broadening its activities to take leadership in this field, and we are confident that ... we can develop air conditioning as it should be developed for the benefit of the public." [22]

American Blower Corporation, an AR&SS subsidiary, was founded in 1881 in Detroit, Michigan, with the invention of a special exhaust fan. By 1931, it produced a variety of air conditioning systems for heating, cooling and ventilation.

Air conditioning had been introduced to large office buildings in the early twenties, however, and the company appeared to have gotten into business too late. The division was shut down 10 years later.

On February 13, 1934, Theodore Ahrens, then 75, retired as president of American Radiator & Standard Sanitary Corporation, though he would remain on the company's executive committee and board of directors. Illness prompted Ahrens to step down, and he subsequently moved to Florida for his health.[23] Woolley assumed Ahrens' responsibilities, and it would fall to him to keep the merged company afloat as the Depression wore on.

The American economy showed signs of stirring by the middle of the decade, though it would not fully rebound until World War II. Many of President Franklin Roosevelt's reforms, intended to spur construction, benefited construction-dependent companies like American Radiator & Standard Sanitary. In 1934, for example, the repair-loans provisions of the National Housing Act — part of Roosevelt's New Deal — went into effect. Homeowners could borrow between $100 and $2,000 for renovations and improvements, in notes payable over three years. The government guaranteed up to 20 percent of the loan.

So crucial were these reforms that they won Roosevelt an endorsement on the eve of the 1934 congressional elections from the normally conservative Clarence Woolley. "I have always been a rank Republican, but I take my hat off to President Roosevelt. The Administration has performed a miracle," he publicly announced, confounding Republican Party leaders, who counted on his support to stage a last-minute attack on the New Deal.

"Woolley ... issued a statement to the press that made the front page of great Democratic journals and must have raised a chorus of groans at G.O.P. headquarters. The statement was ... breezy, swingy, and juicily phrased, good headline stuff. Mr. Woolley was merely giving public thanks for one of the many instances in which the New Deal has given direct aid to Old Deal institutions. The 'miracle' to which he referred was a partial feeding, underwritten by the government, of his long-starved elephant, American Radiator & Standard Sanitary Corp." [24]

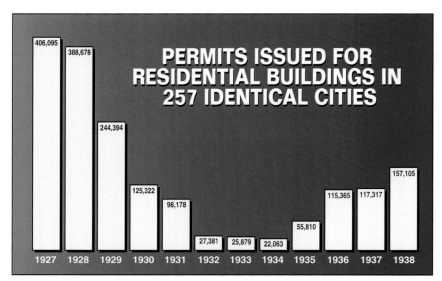

1927	1928	1929	1930	1931	1932	1933	1934	1935	1936	1937	1938
406,095	388,678	244,394	125,322	98,178	27,381	25,879	22,063	55,810	115,365	117,317	157,105

PERMITS ISSUED FOR RESIDENTIAL BUILDINGS IN 257 IDENTICAL CITIES

This graph shows the dramatic decline in home construction compared to the boom years of the 1920s.

But Woolley had reason to be grateful. In the first 60 days of the loan program, sales had jumped 40 percent compared with the same period in the previous year. "Friends ask us if we are holding an auction. We are. We're selling the Depression out of existence,"[25] countered Woolley. In 1934, the company showed a profit of $1.5 million, compared to $881,575 the previous year. "Largely as a result of the activity stimulated by this Act, we are able to report encouraging net profits for the year. To emerge from red into the realm of black figures is indeed most gratifying."[26]

Woolley remained politically active through the Depression years. He supported federal assistance for home loans; a minimum wage requirement; and the revision or abolition of laws like the Sherman Antitrust Act, which he believed hindered the growth of an industrial economy. "I believe," he was quoted in *The New York Times* on April 11, 1935, "that if our friends in Washington were to come out tomorrow morning and say, 'We are considering the advisability of stabilizing currency at an early date and are not contemplating any plans for further devaluation,' you would see prosperity snap back in this country to a degree that would be a delight and joy to every American citizen."[27]

Those who were lucky enough to have jobs worked hard to keep them. Annabelle Christie, who celebrated 62 years with American Standard in 1998, was hired during the Depression. (As of early 1999 she was still working as secretary to Emmanuel Kampouris, president, chairman and CEO of American Standard.) When hired, she worked for American Radiator. Interviewed in 1998, Christie recalled how she had to know the data on every product and perform several different functions. One of her duties was to determine which warehouse to ship product from when an order arrived. "I spent a lot of hours using a slide rule," she said. She also had to inspect radiator sections as they were unloaded. "When a railroad car came in with product, I had to go out there and see it before they unpacked it."[28]

Research and Development

The Depression didn't hamper the company's "search for new products and for equivalent products at lower prices."[29] By 1935, access to raw materials had improved and new machinery and labor procedures had increased employee output. When American Radiator first began producing appliances in 1888, a laborer could produce three units in an hour and earn 10 cents for doing so. By 1935, a worker could produce 16 units an hour and earn 70 cents.[30]

In 1934, the Neo-Angle bath made its debut. The tub was designed with small homes in mind and featured two seats at opposite corners of the tub. The tub was successful beyond the company's expectations and became the top choice of builders, and the factories were hard pressed to meet the demand. It was "modern, elegant, utilitarian and utilized every square inch of space," the company catalog said.[31]

Disunited Union

American Radiator & Standard Sanitary had more than bad economic times to contend with, as seething internal rivalries threatened the company's survival. "Mr. Woolley's optimism encourages him to believe he will emerge with his usual success ... but there are some who feel doubtful," *Fortune* stated in 1935. "They believe the elephant that took so sick almost the minute it was born in 1929 must radically change its mode of life if it hopes to maintain a commanding position in a changed world."[32]

No real thought had been given to uniting the two companies in spirit or goals. Though legally joined, the companies and their subsidiaries continued to work as they always had — separately. Once the papers were signed, Woolley returned to his New York skyscraper and to his first love, the radiator business. He was in the midst of upgrading some of the factories when demand fell off and the new machinery became a liability, so much so that one of the newly revamped plants was closed. Radiators were losing ground to the warm-air furnace, which was coming into vogue as the preferred method of heating in new houses. Woolley remained steadfast in his faith in the radiator and spent nearly $1 million per year on advertising, but American Radiator's domestic sales nevertheless fell off while Standard Sanitary's remained strong.

The conflict, which would hobble the company for 10 years, trickled down from the board room to the factory line. In Newark, American Radiator built a warehouse next to one used by Standard Sanitary. Standard Sanitary then erected a fence between them, forcing American Radiator workers to construct their own driveway and entrance. In Philadelphia, Standard Sanitary employees asked their counterparts at American Radiator to walk around the building rather than take a shortcut through "their" side.[33]

Even worse, the various subsidiaries competed with each other to the detriment of all. American Radiator had purchased Fox Furnace Company of Elyria, Ohio, manufacturer of a new kind of oil-fired furnace. But rather than building sales for the new affiliate, the parent company's salesmen promoted radiators as more hygienic and efficient. The subsidiary fought back by aggressively marketing furnaces as "winter air conditioning." With effective marketing for the new product, Fox drove its sales — and consequently that of its competitors — up. "So, in the end ... it not only fortified its own position but aided the furnace industry to invade the field of cast-iron radiation."[34]

Meanwhile, Standard Sanitary, still based in Pittsburgh, was the "resentful underdog," even though both it and American Radiator were the principal subsidiaries of the holding company. President Henry Reed disliked Woolley's free-spending ways and hands-off management style. Reed "spoke bluntly about the extravagance," a magazine article would later note.

"When he told his Standard salesmen there would be no bonus a certain year, he could not help adding that a great deal of money was needed to keep American Radiator's radio program on the air. Having an unspeakably low opinion of that program, the plumbing salesmen howled and spread the bad word. The antagonism was completely ramified. The employees still talk about it."[35]

Above: The Neo-Angle bath became the top choice of builders when it was introduced in 1934.

Right: Fox Furnace Company produced the venerable Sunbeam warm-air heating furnace.

Not only did American Radiator and Standard Sanitary operate as separate entities, but so did their subsidiaries. It was not unusual for six salesmen representing various divisions of the parent company to call on the same contractor or jobber all in one day.

A Takeover Attempt

In 1937, Reed and other leaders at Standard tried to buy the company. The attempt failed, but Woolley's means of dealing with his most powerful critic "was to give him the job to do himself," *Fortune* magazine noted. Woolley offered Reed the job, which he accepted, and in 1938 the 78-year-old Woolley stepped down as chief executive of the combined companies.

The company's structure was already changing even as Reed moved to take the reins. Woolley had already decided to truly merge the leadership, assets and functions of American Radiator and Standard Sanitary. In addition to streamlining operations, Woolley was also looking for a way to abolish the holding company because of changes in

tax laws. He wrote to shareholders that legislation enacted by the 1936 session of Congress encouraged him to consider dissolving the holding company in favor of an operating company.

"Under existing tax laws pertaining to Holding Companies, there is a double taxation on dividends, that is to say, if the American Radiator Company declares and pays a dividend to the Holding Company, it will be obliged to pay a tax of $2\,^1/_4$ percent thereon, whereas if our Holding Company is set up as an operating company, this tax can be saved."[36]

Dissolving the Holding Company

Reed acted quickly as he assumed the helm of the badly disjointed company. "He automatically dispensed with many men who had been close to Mr. Woolley," *Fortune* magazine reported. Reed fired Arthur Herske, American Radiator sales vice president, who had been Mr. Woolley's choice as his successor, and replaced him with the churchgoing Martin J. Beirn, who had been sales manager before Mr. Herske.[37]

Reed then tackled the formidable job of integrating the organization into one operating company, "probably saving a million a year in taxes, salaries, sales effort, etc. It is said that when he gets done, Mr. Reed may have saved between $3 million to $4 million a year all told."[38]

On January 31, 1939, American Radiator and Standard Sanitary, the biggest subsidiaries of the holding corporation (officially called American Radiator & Standard Sanitary Corporation), were dissolved. The holding company became the operating company, and the 25 subsidiaries were reduced to 12 operating divisions, with the major trade names left intact. Trusted brand names such as American Blower Corporation, C.F. Church Company, the Detroit Lubricator Company, Kewanee Boiler Corporation, Ross Heater & Manufacturing Company and the Tonawanda Iron

---

Clarence Woolley's optimism during the darkest days of the Great Depression prompted *Fortune* magazine to declare he had "a depression-proof psychology."

CLARENCE M. WOOLLEY

CLARENCE WOOLLEY'S RESOLUTE character was forged early in life on the anvil of personal loss. Woolley suffered the loss of his privileged lifestyle as the son of a wealthy Detroit banker and iron manufacturer and several years later suffered a more tragic loss when his father died.

Woolley's unbridled enthusiasm and self-confidence brought him success in just a few years, however. Perhaps his experiences in life taught Woolley the importance of enjoying life. His business trips abroad, for example, became a lifelong source of entertainment and pleasure. Woolley loved the finer things in life, the music, the liquors and the architecture of the various European countries he visited.

Although probably one of the richest men in the Greenwich, Connecticut, area, Woolley was

Any business position seriously entered upon is the threshold of a great adventure.

— Clarence M. Woolley[1]

not part of its social scene and by most accounts did not seem to be particularly well-known. Woolley lived on the 22-acre estate Sunridge Farm on the outskirts of town and owned a home in New Mexico that he visited once a year. His sons, J. Carrington and Clarence Mott Woolley, Jr., spent summers in New Mexico, and J. Carrington settled there as an adult. Woolley also had a daughter, Doriane, whom he once referred to as a "limousine-type radical" while she was attending Bennington College.

Woolley was a collector of furniture and art. In his Connecticut home hung a portrait of his wife, Isabelle Baker Woolley, painted by the famous and controversial artist Salvador Dali. The portrait includes "a small male nude scampering off into the background." Gary Melchers, an American master painter and Woolley's childhood friend, painted a portrait of Woolley, also on display in the Connecticut house. In addition to his love of architecture and art, Woolley was a voracious reader — consuming biographies of powerful men — and an appreciator of music, from ragtime to Bach.[2]

During his lifetime, Woolley sat on the boards of directors of two railroads and six corporations including General Motors, General Electric and Johns-Manville. He was also the director of the Federal Reserve Bank of New York.

Following his dispute with Reed, Woolley retired in 1938, spending his summers at Laguna Beach, California. It was here that he died on July 18, 1956. His son J. Carrington and two grandsons survived Clarence Woolley. They — along with a handful of friends and former employees, four educational institutions and several charities — were the beneficiaries of his $750,000 estate.[3]

Corporation would remain on their respective products. Likewise, the divisions' operating departments were consolidated in Pittsburgh, although the executive offices remained in Manhattan.

Unlikely Competition

An unlikely new competitor emerged as American Radiator & Standard Sanitary pulled itself together. The rise of direct-to-customer merchants and catalog giants like Sears, Roebuck & Company threatened to cut out the middle man, in this case the master plumbers who installed Standard Sanitary's products. Sears, which supplied the homeowner with a book of instructions and loaned him a set of tools at no cost, estimated its appliance sales at $100 million per year.

The National Association of Master Plumbers fought back in trade publications and vilified General Robert E. Wood, president of Sears, who the association claimed used his Washington connections unfairly:

"Let's take a look at that ubiquitous monger of fly-pie, that thousand-handed seller of pretzel on a stick — the modern mail-order house. To us it is plain as day that the so-called mail order houses are disorganizers of industry, profiteering monopolies, vendors of much low-grade cheap merchandise and political manipulators. ... Whenever there's a tough economic knot to cut in Washington, they send for the General. With his shining sword he cuts it dexterously and returns to his regular job at Sears. ... In peace or in war, you'll always find General Wood sitting close to the throne with his foot in the aisle for us."[39]

While he did not publicly rebuke direct-to-you sellers, Reed asserted that his company's

The Tonawanda Iron Division, located on the Niagara River in New York, supplied iron ore to the parent company's plants all over the country.

merchandise was considerably better than what the consumer could buy direct. He also adopted a price-cutting strategy that he believed would allow the company to best the mail-order houses and produce profits in the bargain.

While fighting the direct-to-you trend was obviously a priority, Reed had also to contend with old-line competitors, but here his skills were more practiced. "It is a pleasant feeling to live among gentlemen, even to oppose them in combat. Kohler and Crane are largest and there are many small manufacturers. They know their places and harbor no ambition to conquer the world."[40]

There was also the challenge of new technology. Using a revolutionary new process, Briggs Manufacturing Company, a competitor, turned out "Beautyware" formed-metal plumbing fixtures. While dry enamel was fused onto the metal in traditional cast-iron fixtures, formed-metal fixtures offered many advantages. Colors in a wider spectrum could be sprayed onto these fixtures at room temperature before they were baked, and they weighed a third less than iron tubs and sinks. Their lighter weight made them easier to install and cheaper to mass-produce.

While fending off new competition, Reed continued to reorganize the company, trim unnecessary expenses and promote unity. By 1940, Reed had consolidated the sales staff and combined the individual catalogs for American Radiator and Standard Sanitary.[41]

Reed's reorganization efforts would get sidetracked by World War II. But the war would go further in uniting American Radiator & Standard Sanitary than ever before, and the company would prove indispensable to the war effort.

Many a heart is yearning

Many are the hearts that are yearning for loved ones far away — in service some-where — on land, in the air, on the sea, or underneath. It becomes the patriotic duty of every American without exception, to work unceasingly, to contribute without stint, to sacrifice without restraint, to pray fervently for our righteous cause, to the end that complete victory be achieved and lonely hearts be reunited in a lasting Peace.

Henry M. Reed
CHAIRMAN

The above message was published in full color in December 26 Saturday Evening Post and January 9, 1943 Collier's Also in 297 daily newspapers and as a lithographed poster in full color. Circulation in excess of 24,000,000 copies.

With its factories converted to wartime production and civilian production halted, AR&SS advertised hope during World War II.

CHAPTER FOUR

THE WAR YEARS

1939–1945

"The products to which we devoted our peacetime energies are essential to human health and comfort and helped increase the span of life. But War imposed new and urgent needs which all industry had to meet. The needs of both Peace and War could not be combined and supplied at the same time."

— American Radiator & Standard Sanitary advertisement, 1943[1]

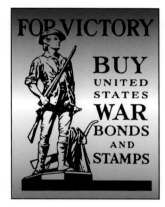

THE GREAT DEPRESSION HAD left its mark on the American psyche as a time of deprivation and uncertainty, but the effects of the worldwide depression had led to revolution in Europe. Italy had fallen under the fascist control of Benito Mussolini in 1925; an inflation-wracked Germany, still simmering with resentment after its defeat in World War I, turned to Adolf Hitler's glowing promises of glory. Following the Spanish Civil War, Spain too became fascist.

American Radiator & Standard Sanitary Corporation was caught in the middle of the growing threat of war because it maintained factories along with affiliated companies in all these nations as well as France, Belgium and Switzerland. The plants produced items meant to improve the health and welfare of the world but used the very materials and tools needed to wage war: various metals and the tools with which to shape and work metal into arms, armor and ammunition.

In March 1938 Hitler forced what became known as the *Anchluss* (union) with Austria, where another American Radiator & Standard Sanitary plant was located. By the end of the year currency restrictions were in effect. By then, Chairman Henry Reed had removed operations and assets of the German and Italian plants and subsidiaries from the year-end balance sheet. The company ended 1938 with $109.3 million in sales. (The German and Italian subsidiaries would have contributed $11.3 million to the consolidated balance sheet.)

World War II began in Europe on September 1, 1939, when Germany invaded Poland. Two days later, Great Britain and France declared war on Germany.

The Second World War

Poland fell within a month. The United States again tried to stay out of the world conflict, and debate raged between interventionists and isolationists. But in 1940, after months of relative inactivity, Germany launched the blitzkrieg. Countries not involved in the fighting were attacked and quickly defeated in rapid succession — Denmark, Norway, Belgium and the Netherlands. France fell on June 14, after its supposedly impregnable Maginot line was outflanked when German troops overran Belgium.

Workers were encouraged to buy Liberty Bonds to support the war effort.

Ideal-Standard helped fund research that led to the development of the famous Spitfire, which broke the Luftwaffe's aerial assault in the Battle of Britain. (*Photo courtesy of* Air Force Magazine.)

Americans employed overseas by American Radiator & Standard Sanitary returned home at the war's outset. Military censorship blocked most information from subsidiaries in the occupied territories, but it was believed that factories in the various nations had only suffered minor damage from the war. Henry Reed reported to stockholders that the subsidiaries appeared to be functioning on a "restricted basis."

Great Britain stood alone under sustained German air raids in the Battle of Britain, and the United States rushed war munitions to the beleaguered island. Congress enacted the first peacetime draft in history, and American industry began to convert to wartime production.

Henry Reed pledged to help in America's sudden mobilization in any way possible. Two American Radiator & Standard Sanitary subsidiaries were

1939 — World War II begins in Europe.

1940 — Legal action by the Justice Department against Henry Reed is postponed until after the war.

1939

1940 — AR&SS begins converting some factories to prepare for war.

converted to produce arms, while the rest began supplying plumbing and heating products for defense construction. The company adopted a policy for employees who either enlisted or were drafted into the military. Employees were granted a leave of absence without pay during military service (for a maximum of one year, 40 days), paid one month's salary or wages if they had been with the company for at least a year and permitted to continue their group life insurance. By the end of 1940, 27 American Radiator & Standard Sanitary employees had entered military service and were eligible for the benefits plan.[2]

The Eve of Battle

The year 1940 marked the first full year of operations following the dissolution of the holding company and its subsidiaries to form American Radiator & Standard Sanitary Corporation. Sales had increased to $117.5 million at a greater profit (from $3.7 million in 1939 to $7.3 million) because of the economies and efficiencies realized from merging into a single operating entity. Some of the smaller subsidiaries — among them American Blower Corporation, California Pipe & Supply Company, the Church Manufacturing Company, the Detroit Lubricator Company, Humphreys Coal & Coke Company, Kewanee Boiler Corporation, Ross Heater & Manufacturing Company, Inc., and the Tonawanda Iron Corporation — were merged into the operating company. The number of employees increased from 16,500 to 19,800.[3]

But Reed's accomplishments were overshadowed by Congress' sweeping investigation into violations of the Sherman Antitrust Act allegedly committed by industries, trade associations and labor unions.[4] The committee set up by Congress found "few if any monopolies in the dictionary sense of that term," reported *The New York Times.* But the committee noted that the prevailing industrial set-up — two or more large manufacturers in a given field, with each holding a significant percentage of the business — has a dominating influence on prices and often on the composition of the industry.[5]

The investigation resulted in the indictment of 102 defendants, comprising manufacturers, wholesalers, master plumbers, journeymen plumbers and various associations. Reed and two vice presidents, Frank Kaulback and John Hall, were among those indicted. They were

1943 — AR&SS virtually halts civilian production.

1945

1941 — Rationing of scarce materials begins. AR&SS subsidiaries in occupied Europe fall under enemy control.

1945 — Atomic bombs are dropped on Japan, ending the war.

charged as co-conspirators for adhering to a system of distribution "whereby plumbing supplies are sold by the manufacturer to the wholesaler and resold by the wholesaler to the master plumber who installs them."

Reed and his officers pleaded not guilty to the charges. In the annual report, Reed wrote that "the indictment declares that the method of distribution complained of is arbitrary and not so economical as that whereby the manufacturer sells either direct to the consumer or to retail outlets, such as mail order houses and department stores, selling direct to the public."

"The method of distribution ... has existed in the plumbing industry for generations. Your Corporation believes in it, not as the result of any conspiracy or agreement with others, but solely by choice, because it believes this system is the most efficient and economical method of serving the consumer and the best method of protecting and furthering public health and safety."[6]

The trial was expected to start in 1940 but was postponed by the need for American industry to pull together for mobilization.

American Radiator & Standard Sanitary was uniquely equipped to supply the armed forces with critical parts and munitions of all types when the United States entered the war. By 1943 the company virtually halted the manufacture of peacetime products.

Our war production program

Guns, Tanks, Planes and Ships are composed of many parts, each of which must be made to withstand unusual stress and strain so that the completed unit will function as planned.

We are producing a large variety of these vital parts. Due to the wide diversity of our peace time products, we were equipped for immediate production of many speedily needed parts and devices.

Where plant and equipment conversion was necessary to fit our facilities to the specialized needs of the War Production Program, that step was undertaken with all possible dispatch, and production is now rolling off the line in large volume.

From the start many of our normal products keyed into the War Program without change and we supplied large quantities for the construction and equipment of Army camps, cantonments, hospitals, housing, airports, warships, submarines, cargo vessels and other Army, Navy, Air Force and Maritime requirements. Such products will continue to be supplied on orders emanating from those sources.

We have marshalled our manufacturing facilities and manpower to contribute 100% to Victory and all units are participating, from the production of coke and pig iron to vital parts and complete units.

Use It Up, Wear It Out, Make It Do or Do Without

By 1941, the nation's leaders knew that it was only a matter of time before the United States would join the fury of war, but their attention was focused on Europe. On the morning of December 7, more than 360 Japanese dive bombers, torpedo bombers and fighters swooped out of the clouds to attack the U.S. Navy docked at Pearl Harbor, which was still operating under peacetime con-

ditions. By the end of the attack, five battleships and 14 other vessels were either sunk or heavily damaged. More than 2,000 military personnel and about 400 civilians were killed in the attack. The United States declared war against the Axis powers (Germany, Italy and Japan) within four days.

The attack ended the debate over neutrality as the pace of mobilization speeded up. President Roosevelt called for the production of 60,000 aircraft, 45,000 tanks and 8 million tons of merchant shipping. A War Production

Board was immediately created to oversee the allocation of resources, and government contracts overtook civilian orders. Conservation measures were enacted in any case; the availability of many civilian goods — including plumbing fixtures — quickly dried up in the rush to turn out products for the war effort.

By November 1942, civilian durable goods had been severely restricted. A *New York Times* Sunday supplement detailed the effect of rationing room by room. The supplement made special mention of plumbing and heating fixtures because they require so much metal and rubber:

> *"Plumbing and heating fixtures, because of the high temperature they must endure, are among the household appurtenances requiring metal almost more than any others, but manufacturers of both have cooperated with the War Production Board to save large quantities of iron, steel, brass and copper, as well as chromium, for the war effort. They have done this by reducing production ... and halting the manufacture of many plumbing fixtures."* [7]

The War Production Board had ordered that metal could not be used in plumbing fixtures except for joining hardware or reinforcing mesh; production of sinks stopped, as well as water tanks and wash fountains. Manufacturers had to rely on vitreous china if they wanted to produce these items. Items that required rubber had to use synthetic materials because the nation's rubber supply was critically low.

"For the second time in a little more than a generation the United States again is engaged in total war," Reed somberly declared in the 1941 Annual Report. "How long the war will last, or what its cost will be in human life and destruction, no one can foresee. Victory for our cause must be the outcome of the conflict. In the meantime everything must make way for the war program. Victory is the only thing which counts now."[8] American Radiator & Standard Sanitary devoted most of its capacity to the war effort. A 1943 ad announced that the "needs of both Peace and War could not be combined and supplied at the same time:"

"The products to which we devoted our peacetime energies are essential to human health and comfort, and helped increase the span of life. But War imposed new and urgent needs which all industry had to meet. The needs of both Peace and War could not be combined and supplied at the same time. So, War Production had the call and our factories have been converted largely to producing vital parts for war implements. ... Ordinary

The products to which we devoted our peace-time energies are essential to human health and comfort. Their application to the American way of life helped increase the span of life.

However, war imposed new and urgent requirements which all industry had to meet. Among our facilities devoted to important war production is our Elyria Plant where SUNBEAM Warm Air Equipment was made. It is now devoted entirely to the production of vital magnesium castings for planes, for which there is the greatest need to increase and speed plane output.

After Victory the manufacture of SUNBEAM Warm Air Equipment will be promptly and vigorously resumed. War alone has caused the interruption. Our conception of the post-war period does not call for nor contemplate any change in our pre-war method of distribution.

civilian needs must necessarily await the day when Victory is achieved."[9]

By 1943, more than 70 percent of the company's capacity had been converted for war, and the remaining capacity produced spare parts to keep existing systems running. Facilities such as the Elyria plant, in Ohio, where the Sunbeam warm air furnace had been made, were converted to produce magnesium castings for aircraft. The company became the largest producer of sand mold castings for parts in the Wright engine used in the B-29 Superfortress. Cast magnesium was also used for aircraft landing wheels. Cast iron, cast steel, steel, malleable iron, bronze, copper, brass and aluminum alloy all went to building tanks, tank guns, naval and merchant ships, submarine nets, mines, bombs, shells, temperature controls for use in aircraft, torpedoes, machine guns and Army scout cars.

Individual plants won the coveted Army-Navy "E" Award. The "E" Award originated in 1906 and was given by the Navy commander-in-chief for excellence in gunnery. In later years, the award honored outstanding performance in engineering and communications, and its recipients included plants demonstrating high quality in carrying out Navy contracts. After Pearl Harbor, the award was renamed the Army-Navy Production Award or the Army-Navy "E." The award consisted of a flag to be flown above the plant and a lapel pin for every worker.[10]

The flag soon flew over many American Radiator & Standard Sanitary plants. The Pittsburgh Works, for instance, turned out cast armor for tanks and combat vehicles 90 days ahead of the government schedule. The Baltimore Works became one of the largest producers of tank track shoes, reaching more than 4,000 finished shoes per day.[11] "Whether the war is long or short," wrote

Reed, "we have enlisted for the duration and feel confident that our contribution to the war effort will help bring peace to the world."[12] Four additional plants won the award: Louisville Works, Louisville, Kentucky; Richmond Works, Richmond, California; Elyria Works, Elyria, Ohio; and the Branch House, Chicago, Illinois.

Because most eligible men were serving overseas, the company hired an increasing number of women. Employment reached 20,200, with gross sales rising from $118 million to $152 million.[13]

Under Fire

The European subsidiaries located in enemy-occupied areas were appropriated by German and Italian governments to turn out weapons and ammunition, just as the plants in the Allied nations were converted for war. In an interesting twist of fate, both sides tried to bomb the European plants (owned by American Radiator & Standard Sanitary Corporation) with ordnance very likely made at those plants. "In England during the war, we made bombs in the foundry to drop on the Germans," observed Colin Wise, retired vice president of finance for Ideal Standard Europe. "And the Germans made bombs in their foundry to drop on the British."[14]

Plants in Germany, Italy and German-occupied France were all damaged to one degree or another by American and British bombers. The Britain-based Ideal Boilers & Radiators managed to escape severe physical damage even though Germany had targeted its Hull plant from the outset of the war. The plant had been one of the

Opposite page: The Elyria plant suspended the production of Sunbeam warm air furnaces to produce magnesium castings for aircraft, such as the B-29 Superfortress, below, a strategic long-range bomber. American Radiator & Standard Sanitary built two more plants dedicated to the production of magnesium castings. (*Photo courtesy of* Air Force Magazine.)

Above right: The coveted Army-Navy "E" Award.

TO FIT HEATING AND PLUMBING NEEDS
on ships

AMERICAN HEATING EQUIPMENT

"Standard" PLUMBING FIXTURES

Because of sound, compact design, operating efficiency, dependability and appearance, American Heating Equipment and "Standard" Plumbing Fixtures are installed in ships of all kinds. Typical examples of recent installations are shown in the pictures on this page.

Sales Offices and Branches of the American Radiator & Standard Sanitary Corporation are located in principal cities and they will be glad to furnish you with full information.

AMERICAN RADIATOR & Standard Sanitary
CORPORATION
Marine Fixture Division   •   PITTSBURGH, PA.
Cast Iron & Steel Boilers & Furnaces for Coal, Oil, Gas • Radiators • Cast Iron Enameled & Vitreous China Plumbing Fixtures & Plumbers' Brass Goods • Winter Air Conditioning Units • Coal & Gas Water Heaters • Oil Burners • Heating Accessories

AMERICAN HEATING EQUIPMENT
COST NO MORE THAN OTHERS
"Standard" PLUMBING FIXTURES

In October 1943 the corporation looked optimistically towards a victory that was still two years away.

Luftwaffe's original bombing targets, as evidenced by an aerial photograph that dates back to September 1939 taken by a German reconnaissance plane, and although the surrounding countryside had been hit, the plant was never knocked out of action.

The Hull plant was extremely important to the war effort. The subsidiary turned out 20 million bomb shells and had contributed £5,000 to the Ministry of Aircraft Production to sponsor the development of the Royal Air Force's Spitfire fighter, one of the fastest and most effective single-seat fighters of the war.[15] The Spitfire, combined with the skill of Royal Air Force pilots, defeated the Luftwaffe in 1940 during the Battle of Britain.

Advertising during the War

With few civilian goods to offer, American Radiator & Standard Sanitary's advertising reminded people of the importance of sanitation, heating and plumbing. Other ads dealt with patriotic themes and encouraged people to look to the future. One advertisement depicted a man and woman in uniform looking toward the sky. "Victory is on the horizon," it declared. "With victory on the horizon, now more than ever we must unite in working for, sacrificing for, fighting for and praying for the name which means everything to us, the name which is the beacon light of universal freedom — the greatest name in the world — the United States of America."[16]

The end of the war brought renewed hope that the world could find a way to live in peace, a sentiment echoed in a letter from Henry Reed to shareholders:

> *"Peace. Military victory was won by our gallant men and women, over the most powerful forces ever assembled in the history of the world. Let us hope that the fundamentals fought for will not be lost in the post-war world — not only in the other countries but here at home. Peace and the future will only be what we, as a Nation, make them."*[17]

By the war's end, American Radiator & Standard Sanitary Corporation had produced an amazing amount of ordnance and military products. For example, the company turned out 2.5 million hand grenades, 75 million cast-iron nose pieces for bombs and more than 21 million magnesium bodies for incendiary bombs.[18]

Peace would bring a record-setting demand for new housing, but work stoppages and raw material shortages slowed American industry temporarily. The government canceled millions of dollars in war contracts, which reduced sales 13.6 percent for American Radiator & Standard Sanitary (from $139 million to $120 million).

A total of 5,514 company employees, including 27 women, joined the armed forces and served dur-

ing World War II. Of those, 256 became war casualties — 114 killed, 28 missing and 114 wounded. By December 31, 1945, 1,188 employees had returned to work.[20]

More would soon arrive, however, as Operation Magic Carpet whisked soldiers from Europe to the United States in what President Truman called "the most remarkable demobilization in the history of the world, or 'disintegration' if you want to call it that."[21]

As for the European companies, no useful information could be obtained on the conditions of the German plants, particularly those falling within the Russian zone of occupation. Others sustained damage to one degree or another.

Europe began the hard task of rebuilding its shattered continent. American veterans, meanwhile, returned to a peacetime boom unprecedented in the history of the world.

Joseph Lind of the Louisville Works rests on a pile of granite balls used in the production of bathtub enamel.

CHAPTER FIVE

RETOOLING FOR PEACE
1946–1950

"Nothing has added more to the health and comfort of individuals than the advancement made during this period in heating and sanitation methods, towards which the large volume of new and improved quality products developed by your Company, its predecessors and affiliates, has contributed immeasurably."

— American Radiator & Standard Sanitary 1949 Annual Report[1]

FOR 15 YEARS AMERICANS HAD weathered the greatest economic downturn and the biggest war in history. Flush with money from war bonds and wartime earnings, people were ready to buy again just as soon as civilian goods returned to the shelves.

But the immediate postwar years presented unanticipated challenges for the company. Retooling for peacetime production went easier than expected, but finding workers proved extraordinarily difficult at a time when demand for plumbing and heating goods hit an all-time high. Workers in critical industries such as railroads, steel, mines and petroleum agitated for higher wages and better benefits. President Harry Truman threatened to take over these industries and draft striking union members into the military to run the plants. Price controls were still in effect, and companies like American Radiator & Standard Sanitary sold many of their products at a loss until the controls ended in mid-June.[2]

After years of relatively calm labor relations, workers went on strike at American Radiator & Standard Sanitary in 1945. Critical industries were also hit with strikes, effectively shutting down several of the company's plants. A steel strike in Buffalo in January 1946 kept 1,400 American Radiator Company employees from working until April 26, 1946, when a union agreement was finally reached.[3] At the end of 1946,

workers at the Louisville plant went on a strike, which lasted a month, while the Pittsburgh plant shut down due to a power shortage caused by striking public utility workers. Periodic coal strikes affected a number of company plants.

Meanwhile, demand was "several times the available production," noted the Annual Report. "The Corporation met this crisis by selling these products on the basis of individual customer quotas established for each quarter. This policy, which seemed fair under existing conditions, served to maintain good customer relationships."[4]

American Radiator & Standard Sanitary faced material shortages, price controls, a high labor turnover and inexperienced help. As the government canceled contracts, employment fell from a wartime high of 20,200 in 1942 to just 14,400 workers by 1945. The company absorbed thousands of returning veterans, however, which brought the workforce back to 19,300 a year later.[5]

A postwar economy in transition acted as a backdrop during this period. Canceled wartime government contracts in 1945 had reduced sales

---

For brevity, American Radiator & Standard Sanitary was sometimes shortened to "American-Standard," though the official name remained American Radiator & Standard Sanitary Corporation.

from $139 million to $120 million. Just two years later, sales rebounded to more than $200 million with a workforce topping 23,000 in the United States.

Rebuilding Europe

The European subsidiaries naturally faced more daunting challenges in the Allied-occupied war zones, as the 1945 Annual Report reported.

"The French company, with seven plants, suffered certain war damage, which has been repaired except for one plant that suffered damage to the extent of 30 to 40 percent of its value. ... The Belgian company plant was not damaged, but due to shortage of materials and transportation, the company operated at a relatively low rate of production. ... The Italian company plant at Leghorn was almost completely destroyed."[6]

The German and Austrian companies fared even worse. Little information was available after the war on several of these plants because they fell within the Russian zone of occupation. The Soviet Union carried out its own program of repa-rations for the damage suffered from the German invasion. In some areas, whole factories were shipped out of Germany and rebuilt in the Soviet Union or one of its satellite nations. Company executives determined that the Schoenebeck plant in Germany and the Wiener Neustadt plant in Austria were "being operated under Russian supervision and for Russian benefit."[7] American Radiator & Standard Sanitary Corporation wrote these plants off in 1947 and received a $4.4 million tax refund from the U.S. Treasury for the loss.

As the decade wore on, the remaining European subsidiaries overcame the scarcity of materials and the war damage to help rebuild the continent and even became profitable again.[8]

"Subsidiary companies operating in Belgium, England, France and Switzerland were uniformly affected by shortages of manpower, raw materials and fuel. Despite these difficulties all plants are producing on a fairly satisfactory basis with efficiencies approaching and in some cases exceeding those in the United States, and each company operated on a profitable basis in 1947."[9]

1945-1946 — A wave of labor unrest hits American industry, affecting operations at AR&SS.

1946 — Theodore Mueller is named president; Henry Reed remains chairman.

1945

1945 — European subsidiaries begin to repair war damage. Soviet Union takes over several in its zone of occupation.

A Change in Leader and Focus

After a four-year postponement, the trial for alleged violations of the Sherman Antitrust Act began in November 1946 and was expected to last six to eight months. However, Henry Reed had already resigned as president of the corporation, and no further mention of the suit was made in subsequent annual reports. Reed, who relinquished his role in April, was succeeded by Theodore Mueller, vice president in charge of manufacturing. Though no longer president, Reed remained chairman of the company.

The record does not indicate whether the pending trial had any bearing on Reed's decision, and his health may have been a factor. He died on August 12, 1947, and was memorialized in the 1947 Annual Report:

"He had given life-long service to the Corporation and its predecessors. To each of the many executive positions he occupied, his devotion of his talents, time and energy was unstinting, and in each his contributions to the growth and stability of the Corporation and its predecessors were numerous and far-reaching."[10]

Theodore E. Mueller began his illustrious career at Standard Sanitary's Pittsburgh plant in 1904 as an apprentice pattern maker.

1949 — The company celebrates 50 years in business.

1950

1948 — Sales and income hit record levels as returning veterans create a housing crisis.

1949 — Suburban developments such as Levittown start a rush from the cities, spurring even greater residential construction.

Under Mueller's direction, American Radiator & Standard Sanitary Corporation cut down the number of styles, sizes and types of both heating and plumbing products. The greater standardization cut costs and encouraged the production of high-volume items, such as the new panel radiator.

The subsidiaries, however, continued to develop new products and add to their product lines. The Church Company introduced the "Mot-Tex" toilet seat cover; Ross Heater & Manufacturing Company, Inc., improved its products for marine service and diesel motors; the Kewanee Boiler Corporation introduced a small steel boiler designed especially for moderate-sized homes and small apartment buildings; and the Detroit Lubricator Company developed better temperature controls for home washing machines.[11]

Net sales and income kept climbing. The following year, 1948, set new records with sales of more than $236 million and net income at $26 million. American Radiator & Standard Sanitary Corporation, which began to refer to itself as American-Standard for short, met the ever-rising production demand by modernizing existing plants and opening new facilities. To build more vitreous china, the company purchased and then converted government war surplus property in New Orleans into one of the company's biggest pottery plants.

Located on a 46-acre tract of land, the New Orleans plant employed more than 600 people and produced toilets, lavatories and various other fixtures. The plant's location enabled American-Standard to better supply the South and Southwest with plumbing products.[12]

Orders were up and the company managed to get a handle on its costs and pricing, but plants still suffered from a spotty supply of raw materials. D.D. Couch, vice president and manager of sales at American-Standard, told a *New York Times* reporter that the increased plant capacity was useless without these raw materials:

"Capacity to produce even more than in 1947 is there, and we can utilize the facilities of our plants to the fullest if we obtain the raw and semi-fabricated materials we must have to make heating equipment and plumbing fixtures. The principal shortages that threaten us are in pig iron and sheet steel. If we can get a sufficient supply of them, we can swing into the program we have outlined."[13]

The normal relationship of supply and demand returned the following year. Several plants were temporarily shut down because of a sudden slack in demand and high inventory. The downturn was also temporary; it served as a breather for what would become the largest residential building boom in history.[14]

The Beginning of the Boom

The housing industry suffered the most throughout the war but gained the most with the coming of peace. Millions of veterans discharged from the military had gotten married and were producing the phenomenon called "The baby boom." The housing shortage had become so tight it was literally a crisis. More than 50,000 people lived in surplus Army Quonset huts for lack of housing. In Chicago, trolley cars were used to house several hundred people. Housing starts leaped from the paltry 114,000 for single homes in 1944 to more than 1.7 million by 1950.[15] A man named Bill Levitt, a veteran, had recognized that young families just starting out would leap to own the American Dream at an affordable price. While stationed overseas, he developed a plan to mass-produce homes as part of a huge, pre-planned community called Levittown. Historian David Halberstam wrote that Levitt signed 1,400 contracts the day his office opened in March 1949.[16]

With the economic future of the company and the country looking optimistic, Mueller again announced that American-Standard Corporation was launching a multimillion expansion program. Under the $15 million plan the company acquired new plants and enlarged existing facilities. Since the end of the war, the company had spent $22 million to retool and expand its plants.[17]

The Half-Century Mark

The year 1949 marked the 50-year anniversary of the founding of the forerunners to American Radiator & Standard Sanitary Corporation, which was reflected in the 1949 Annual Report.

Visitors at the New Orleans Works open house inspect water closets ready for final tests.

BIOGRAPHY OF THEODORE E. MUELLER

THEODORE E. MUELLER WAS THE grandson of Theodore Ahrens, Sr., who founded the manufacturing firm of Ahrens & Ott in Louisville in 1862 (see Chapter Two). Born on April 3, 1885, in Louisville, Kentucky, Mueller began working for Standard Sanitary's Pittsburgh plant in 1904 as an apprentice pattern maker, working 12-hour days and earning 50 cents a day. At night, Mueller studied engineering and mechanical drawing at the Carnegie Institute of Technology. He was transferred in 1907 to the Louisville plant where he became the first plant manager. In Louisville, he took mechanical engineering courses through the International Correspondence School. In 1909, he became plant superintendent, and in 1913 he became plant manager. (He held this position until 1928, when he was elected vice president, general manager of factories.) On June 10, 1916, Mueller married Pattie C. Johnston.[1]

Although Mueller made his home on a 400-acre farm outside Louisville named Shady Brook, he commuted to Pittsburgh, and sometimes New York, during the work week and only spent weekends at home. Still, Mueller loved his 20-room estate, which included five baths, and refused to live closer to Pittsburgh. When

he died at the age of 72, one obituary estimated that he had logged over 1 million miles (1.6 million actually) commuting just between Louisville and Pittsburgh. One report said Mueller was well-known by all the porters, conductors, trainmen and other employees at the Pittsburgh train station. Upon Mueller's death, Barney, a redcap, said, "I been carrying his bags every Monday morning for 20 years now — and there's no finer gentleman traveler than him."[2] It is said that he rode in Lower Berth 5 for 20 years until the advent of bedroom-cars. Mueller estimated that he had logged even more miles on the train than the newspapers estimated. "I've traveled more than 3 million miles on the Pennsylvania Railroad alone, and I don't know how many on the other lines. I've never tired of train travel either. I rest well on trains."[3] The *Pittsburgh Post-Gazette* called him the city's Number One Commuter.

On his farm, Mueller carried out his main hobby of breeding thoroughbred horses and blooded stock. Although he always owned horses, Mueller is said never to have bet on a race. He was adamant about not allowing his hobbies to interfere with work. "I've either got to work or play. I can't do both."[4] One of his horses, Pittsburgher, finished second in the $50,000 American Derby in Chicago in 1931. At Shady Brook Farm, Mueller also raised pure-bred Jersey cows, pedigreed Great Danes, Fox Terriers and Muscovy ducks. He also collected antique bath fixtures dating back to the Revolutionary War era.

In 1935 Mueller became a director and member of the executive committee of American Radiator & Standard Sanitary Corporation. He was elected vice president and general manager of manufacturing in 1939 when the company became an operating company. (From the time of the 1929 merger until 1939, the firm had operated as a holding company.) In 1946, Mueller was elected president of the company. Under his leadership, the company began to expand and sales reached record highs. In 1952, Mueller attended the dedication of a $1 million addition to Standard's Brescia, Italy, plant. At the plant

opening, Mueller was awarded the Order of the Star of Solidarity by the Italian government for his role in reconstructing the nation's industry. A few years earlier, in 1949, he was honored by a marching band during a trip to Belgium, where Standard had a pottery plant.

When he died of a heart attack on September 24, 1957, Mueller held the position of director emeritus. Having suffered a stroke during a stockholders' meeting in 1953, Mueller was no longer able to remain active in the company, but his affection never waned. He once said of the company's 30,000 workers: "They are not only my fellow employees, but my best friends."

"Nothing has added more to the health and comfort of individuals than the advancement made during this period in heating and sanitation methods, towards which the large volume of new and improved quality products developed by your Company, its predecessors and affiliates, has contributed immeasurably.

"We have progressed from the days of the kitchen washtub and outhouse to the bathroom, with its modern bathtub, shower, lavatory and toilet; from homes and buildings insufficiently heated, largely by stoves, to a modern heat distribution unit, automatically controlled, consisting of a boiler with various kinds of new and improved radiation; or a warm air furnace with its conditioning features; or unit heaters, etc.; from the teakettle to the automatic water heater; from the table dishpan to the Hostess sink and kitchen cabinet." [18]

Together with its subsidiary companies, American-Standard operated 28 plants around the world by 1949; its affiliated companies operated another 11. In 50 years, the company and its predecessors had sold 7 million heating boilers, hundreds of thousands of warm air furnaces, 14 million bath-

Above: This miniature bathroom was a design study prepared by the Louisville Works. But Mary Ann Bonn liked it better as a toy.

Below: American-Standard Institute of Heating Research in Louisville, Kentucky, where the company consolidated its research facilities.

tubs, 15 million enamel cast-iron sinks, more than 20 million lavatories and 15 million water closets.

The company maintained research laboratories in Detroit, Michigan; Yonkers, New York; Louisville, Kentucky; and several cities in Europe. During the war, research had centered on becoming more efficient, but attention once again focused on improving sanitation and heating products. The research staff was beefed up, and a consolidated facility in Louisville was designed and built for all domestic heating and plumbing product development.[19]

Consolidated net sales in 1950 reached the record-breaking mark of $289 million, which represented a 38 percent increase over 1949. Backlog orders hit their highest in the history of the corporation.

But just as the economy shifted fully to peacetime, the Cold War spread across the world. By

Above left: An enameler at the Louisville Works dusts hot iron bathtubs with a coat of enamel.

Above right: After the enamel cools, a worker pounds the material with a rawhide hammer to make sure the enamel adheres to the hot iron.

1949, Americans received a double shock: Communists in China had defeated the Nationalists, and the Soviet Union exploded its first atomic bomb, ending the monopoly held by the United States.

In June 1950, soldiers from communist North Korea crossed the 38th parallel, sweeping across South Korea, located close to American-occupied Japan. The company prepared to once again answer the call to arms as the economy shifted back to a wartime footing.

An explosion in military and civilian demand kept foundries working overtime. Here, a long row of flasks at the Bond plant receives molten iron.

CHAPTER SIX

THE BOOMING FIFTIES

1951–1959

"It doesn't leave much room for improvement, does it?"

— Joseph A. Grazier, 1953[1]

Meet...

THE
AMERICAN-Standard
FAMILY

THE OUTBREAK OF THE Korean War brought wartime controls to the economy again, and raw materials were once more restricted for military use. After much fighting, forces under Gen. Douglas MacArthur were near victory, pushing well beyond the 38th parallel into Korea, and toward China, when thousands of Chinese soldiers swept across the border. With American forces falling back, President Truman declared a national emergency in December 1950.[2]

The federal Controlled Materials Plan was enacted, restricting the availability of raw materials, while the Office of Defense Mobilization put the economy back on a war footing. Responding to an urgent request by the government, American-Standard converted two of its plants to produce magnesium castings for aircraft. The Litchfield and Pittsburgh plants, which had produced heating and cast-iron enamel plumbing, respectively, avoided layoffs due to a slowdown in construction by converting to defense-related production. About 30 percent of goods produced by the company's subsidiaries were soon defense-related.[3]

Executives still had reason to be optimistic because the company, like many industries, had entered a remarkable period of growth catering to both civilian and military needs. "Few industrialists have made better use of the postwar boom than [President] Theodore E. Mueller has," stated a 1951 *Business Week* magazine article. "Behind the fast growth, of course, was a 15-year unfilled demand dating from Depression and war years. American-Standard expanded right along with the postwar housing boom."[4]

Writing to shareholders, Mueller agreed:

"While the impact of defense restrictions may cause some decrease in the sales of non-defense items during 1952, we are confident about the long-range prospects. ... Population studies based on 1950 census figures ... indicate a need of approximately one million new residential units annually with this minimum figure, increasing annually in the next decade."[5]

In just six years, the company's sales had risen 154 percent, from $120 million in 1945 to $305 million in 1951.[6] That year, American Radiator & Standard Sanitary shortened its name to American-Standard. Products, advertisements, plants and buildings would no longer bear the longer, more

---

American-Standard published an introductory brochure in 1952 to introduce its family of four domestic subsidiaries and 12 affiliated companies in Canada and Europe to the public.

In 1951, American-Standard purchased Acme Metal Products, of Dover, New Jersey, a maker of steel kitchen cabinets.

cumbersome name. American-Standard would become one of the world's key manufacturer by the end of the decade. Operating in 11 countries, it produced plumbing, heating and a host of other products including refrigeration units, kitchen appliances, automatic controls, molded plastic parts, navigation devices, radar components and a number of classified products for the military.

A Surprise in the Kitchen

An exodus from the city to the new, pre-planned residential suburbs began in 1950. By 1955, these new subdivisions "represented 75 percent of the new housing starts," wrote historian David Halberstam in the book *The Fifties*: "All over America, subdivisions were advertising

1951 — American-Standard converts two plants back to wartime production for the Korean War.

1953 — Joseph Grazier becomes president of American-Standard.

1951

1951 — Acme Metal Products, maker of steel kitchen cabinets, is purchased.

1955 — Atomic Energy Division is established.

that buyers could come in for no down payment and others were asking 'one dollar down.' ... It would change the nature of American society."[7]

It also spurred American-Standard to move more deeply into other parts of the house. In 1951, Acme Metal Products, a manufacturer of steel kitchen cabinets, was purchased and merged a year later. By the middle of the decade, American-Standard had purchased the $170 million Mullins Manufacturing Corporation and merged its packaged kitchen line with the Youngstown Kitchens Division.

It was hoped that the combination would boost the company's overall kitchen sales. "For years American Radiator & Standard Sanitary Corporation has had its foot in the kitchen door," asserted *Business Week* magazine. "It has been making kitchen sinks since the day they were invented. Now American-Standard has wiggled all the way into the kitchen."[8]

The division built and distributed some of the most popular steel sinks; steel wall, base and specialty cabinets; automatic electric dishwashers and electric food waste disposers.[9] But the strategy dragged the company back into the courtroom for alleged antitrust violations. Two months following

Combined under the Youngstown Kitchens Division, Acme and later acquisitions produced other kitchen items such as electric food disposal systems and dishwashers.

the Mullins merger, the Department of Justice filed suit against American-Standard for supposedly

1955 — Mullins Manufacturing is purchased.

1959 — Contour bathtub becomes a hit with homeowners.

1959

1957 — European companies become most profitable segment of American-Standard.

1959 — Sales reach $517 million, but income performance falls in the United States.

violating Section 7 of the Clayton Act. The legal action was particularly irksome because the government had received the necessary information prior to the merger and did not object. In a message to shareholders, the company vowed to fight:

"All aspects of the merger, including its propriety under the antitrust laws, had been carefully considered before the action was recommended to stockholders for approval. Prompt announcement was made, therefore, that the Corporation would vigorously defend its position in the courts. An answer has been filed denying the allegations of the complaint, and our attorneys are preparing to defend against them."[10]

But by 1960, with years of litigation still pending, American-Standard accepted a consent decree to end the matter. Retired counsel Frank Berberich, who started with the company in 1947, said the original Acme acquisition was later considered to be the first misstep: "We bought a

relatively large steel kitchen cabinet manufacturer, which impaired our ability to buy a bigger and better one when we wanted to later on."[11]

Mueller continued to consolidate businesses to improve efficiency. Kewanee Boiler Corporation and Ross Heater & Manufacturing Company, Inc., acquired in 1940, were merged into Kewanee-Ross Corporation.[12]

A Urinal of Their Own

One of the more interesting if ultimately unsuccessful products developed in 1951 was Sanistand, a women's urinal. The design seemed revolutionary, and the company had hoped the product would change sanitation standards in women's public restrooms. The company mounted an intensive advertising campaign, claiming:

"Women the country over will soon be talking about a brand-new, revolutionary fixture for women's public restrooms. It's the Sanistand fixture, a woman's urinal, produced by American Radiator & Standard Sanitary Corporation.

"Made of genuine vitreous china, the Sanistand is designed especially to prevent the spread of germs and improve the sanitary conditions

In 1952 Kewanee Boiler Corporation and Ross Heater were merged into Kewanee-Ross Corporation. Below is one of the Ross plants.

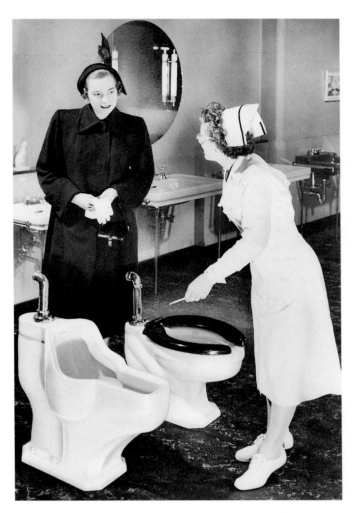

American-Standard may have gone a little too far when it introduced the Sanistand, a urinal designed for women. The product was discontinued.

of women's public restrooms. It need not be touched in usage."[13]

As a pilot program, the Sanistand was placed in public restrooms throughout America — from hotels and railroad stations to department stores to colleges. Company press releases said that the response to the Sanistand was overwhelmingly positive. "Congratulations! It's just what we've always needed — easy to use and very sanitary," was one of the comments the company reported.[14] The majority of women apparently didn't agree, and the Sanistand was quickly discontinued.

Waking Up

From 1953 to 1956 American-Standard broke records in its growth and earnings. "It doesn't leave much room for improvement, does it?" Vice President Joseph A. Grazier once said of his company's track record in 1953.[15] But following Mueller's election as chairman by the board of directors that year, the task of improvement fell to Grazier when he became president.

Born on September 10, 1903, in Tyrone, Pennsylvania, Grazier graduated from Lafayette College in 1925 and earned his law degree from the University of Pennsylvania in 1928. In 1937, he was hired by Clarence M. Woolley to enter the office of the secretary at American Radiator & Standard Sanitary, and he became assistant secretary two years later. He entered the Army in 1942 and served as a lieutenant colonel with the Transportation Corps until his discharge in 1945. After the war, he resumed his post as assistant secretary of American-Standard until 1947, when he became secretary. In 1951, Grazier became vice president and secretary and two years later, president of the company.

Grazier saw that American-Standard had become complacent in its success. "Here was this marvelous, rich, old corporation," recalled Fred Jaqua, who retired as vice president, general counsel in 1996. "It was kind of asleep, but poised to go somewhere."

"And Grazier was a rather dynamic boss who realized that American-Standard had to shake the dust off its feet and do something. We were a terribly well-respected corporation with a huge amount of cash and nothing exciting on its plate."[16]

American-Standard's product line had grown to about a thousand products by the time he took the helm, so Grazier mounted a reorganization effort which began with a "decentralization of responsibility."[17] The Sunbeam Air Conditioner Division was formed to oversee the production of air conditioners and warm-air furnaces. "This was done because the warm-air heating and air conditioning field had developed along lines different from the plumbing and radiator heating field," said Grazier. Similarly, the Amstan Supply

Division was created to oversee the company's wholesale supply houses. "Here again, the circumstances and conditions under which a wholesale distributing organization does business are different from our other fields. It is our belief that increased freedom of action for the branch house will result in more effective operations by them," Grazier said.[18]

In 1954, the company completed the consolidation of its executive offices in New York, and Grazier looked toward the future. He correctly anticipated the growing popularity of central air conditioning and heat. A year later American Blower began producing air conditioning for commercial buildings.

Grazier stepped up the pace. He launched a three-year, $60 million plan to build new facilities and modernize and expand existing plants, while encouraging decentralization, according to a 1954 *Fortune* magazine article:

"*Mr. Grazier's program gives authority and accountability to the heads of American-Standard's nine domestic and foreign divisions. It concentrates in New York the company's headquarters, formerly split between that city and Pittsburgh ... but Mr. Grazier has also done something unique. He has shaped a program to stimulate selling by a group of men whose reputation as merchandisers is poor — the old master plumbers who now are plumbing and heating contractors.*"[19]

Grazier planned to introduce products to the public through "at least one responsible plumber-retailer in every community in the country." To let people see and touch American-Standard products, the company inaugurated storefront shops in target communities.

"*It became clear soon after the close of World War II that sales and market conditions in plumbing and radiator heating were undergoing substantial changes. ... Here again the principle of independent, or decentralized, operation is being followed. Eventually, this should mean more orders for products — more business for our*

Left and above: Ideal Standard opened an elegant showroom in Brussels, Belgium, in 1950. "The general opinion is that this showroom is a success, and we have no doubt it will prove an excellent sales tool," wrote Ideal Standard Managing Director P. Lebrun in a letter to Mueller.

plants because our sales force will be able to move more quickly and certainly, and we hope, more effectively.*[20]

The company had completed the consolidation of its research facilities in Louisville, and in November 1953 the quarterly board of directors meeting was held there. During a tour of the Louisville facilities, Grazier remarked that advanced equipment was useless without good people to operate it:

"American-Standard has progressed from that little brass foundry which was started here almost a century ago into a large and far-flung — and successful — corporation. Machines and instruments played a part in that progress. And by far the largest part was played by people. That is just as true now as it ever has been. So we have come to Louisville, not only to look at processes and techniques, but also to meet and become better acquainted with you — the men who give meaning and direction to the tools of modern industry."[21]

The people who worked the machines operated in a consistently congenial atmosphere that tended to filter from the president's office on down. Henry Steiner worked for American-

Standard for almost 30 years as an executive. He and other retirees recalled an environment that encouraged rapport: "My wife and I have drawn a great many friends over the years from the people in the company. I think that has existed during all of that period."[22]

The company entered the new field of atomic energy during this period, establishing the Atomic Energy Division in 1955. More of a research area than a profit center, the division did consulting work for the Atomic Energy Commission and supplied some instrumentation for the first commercial atomic power station in the United States, located at Shippingport, Pennsylvania.[23]

With $522 million in sales from both domestic and foreign markets, American-Standard once again broke its sales record in spite of a 16 percent drop in housing starts and several strikes that shut down the heating plants in Buffalo and Louisville. Grazier had a glowing report to present to shareholders at the end of 1956:

"Our whole organization has achieved a vitality, an aggressiveness and a momentum that will not only carry us through the highly competitive period immediately ahead, but also will result in improved sales and earnings in the years to come."[24]

The Interstate Highway Act of 1956 promised to keep the suburban building boom thriving. The largest public works project in American history, the act made commuting to jobs in the city easier and launched the Automobile Age, in which people could travel all over the country in reasonable comfort. Don Feigel, who began his career with American-Standard as a file clerk in 1954 and by 1997 had become a member of the sales and distribution team, recalled the boom days:

"A lot of the big contractors had started developments in Florida. One that stuck in my mind was Bond Plumbing. We were talking in the vicinity of 5,000 to 6,000 tubs on a particu-

A tub pattern used in the Baltimore plant.

American Standard executives toured the Brescia plant in Italy.

lar job release. This was a tremendous amount of paperwork because we ran without computers then."[25]

Sales in foreign markets also hit records because the Old World, still recovering from World War II, had the chance to modernize as it rebuilt. "Due to war damage, normal deterioration and obsolescence, rising living standards and population increases, the demand for housing is not being currently met even with the present high rate of activity," Grazier reported to stockholders. The European subsidiaries once

again rivaled the American market for profitability: "They were proud to be part of American-Standard, but they felt they were the best in American-Standard," explained Colin Wise, retired vice president of finance for Ideal Standard Europe. "They held their own with all their American colleagues."[26]

By 1957, the European companies did more than hold their own; they were the most profitable segment of the company. Although sales in the United States remained relatively healthy, rising costs for labor and raw materials pushed the profit margin down to a scant 2 percent on the dollar. The

Standard employed an "immense industrious army" of workers.[27]

The mayor of Brescia, Italy, and various dignitaries were on hand to meet Grazier and tour the plants, the newspaper reported:

"The group of authorities and engineers began the visit in the heating plant, staying longer in the foundry, where the cupola was vomiting streams of incandescent cast iron. ... They then followed the production line, which shows a time and motion study demanding constant and accurate carefulness from the worker but rewarding him munificently, at levels above the normal ones."[28]

The lackluster performance in the United States was followed by another surge in commercial and residential construction the following year. A new type of urinal was introduced that would gradually edge out the floor model. The urinal was suspended from the wall to make it easier to clean the area around it. New gas and electric water heaters were introduced as well as more efficient heating and cooling units and more durable toilet seats. Kitchen equipment continued to be a focus, and the company offered products that combined steel, wood and plastic to form the basis of the "modern" 1950s-type kitchen. In early 1959, the new Contour bath arrived on the scene, and consumers readily accepted it.

On January 1, 1959, American-Standard formed a new Industrial Division, based in Detroit and headed by John W. Brennan, the former president of the American Blower Division. The new division comprised American Blower, Kewanee Boiler and Ross. These three divisions had similar products and markets, and the company thought the benefits of such a division would include greater marketing power plus engineering and product development.

Net sales for 1959 hit $517 million while net income was $21 million. "We enter the decade of the 1960s with determination and optimism," said Grazier.[29] But his optimism proved short-lived as American-Standard rode a wave of litigation and disappointing domestic income in the sixties.

rise of the European Common Market in the late 1950s helped the overseas companies to expand.

Grazier toured these subsidiaries in 1958. In some places he was treated like an "eminent American general" who was reviewing "one of the many regiments under his command. ... He wore no stripes or decorations, no blare of trumpet was heard on his arrival. ... He just stepped out of a long car and started to shake hands," wrote the local newspaper. The newspaper explained that it considered Grazier a general because American-

Look for the polka dots and you'll find the safer bathtub

Not slippery when wet! When you sit down in this American-Standard bathtub, you do it on purpose! Tests show Stan-Sure* bathtub bottoms are four times safer than conventional tub surfaces. A slip-resistant finish beautiful to look at, comfortable to sit on and easy to clean. No messy tapes or mats. Available on all American-Standard cast iron tubs . . . fused right into the triple-thick enamel. Give your family the extra protection of exclusive Stan-Sure bathtubs. See your American-Standard plumbing contractor (He's listed in the Yellow Pages under "Plumbing Supplies" or "Plumbing Fixtures") or mail the coupon. • TRADEMARK AR&SS CORP.

⊖ **AMERICAN STANDARD**

AMERICAN-STANDARD, Dept. PBH-567
Box 2, Midtown Station,
New York, N.Y. 10018
Please send me your booklet "New Fashion Ideas for Bathrooms."
I enclose 10¢ to cover mailing.
I am modernizing ☐.
I am building ☐.

Name _____
Address _____
City _____ State _____
County _____ Zip No. _____

The skid-resistant bathtub was introduced in 1965 in response to consumer demands for better safety.

CHAPTER SEVEN

TRANSFORMATION– A DECADE OF EXPANSION

1960–1970

"Look at my record. I'm a believer in debt."

— William Eberle, *Fortune* magazine, 1967[1]

THE UNITED STATES ENTERED the sixties with the youthful optimism that helped elect John F. Kennedy, the youngest president up to that time. Magazines such as *Better Homes and Gardens* reflected the sunny, conservative outlook with articles that advised people on how to remodel homes to create a sense of space and modernity. Advertising emphasized convenience and aesthetics, as in this American-Standard ad for the new wall-hung toilet and contoured bathtub:

> *"Each smart product in this bathroom combines new beauty with practical convenience. The off-the-floor toilet lets you swish a mop under it for new ease of cleaning. The Contour bathtub has two ledges and extra room for bathing, thanks to the off-center design. The lavatory design, also off-center, provides a roomy shelf."[2]*

Colors remained relatively restrained and harmonized as well. "Most popular schemes today are scored for ... close harmony," one *Better Homes and Gardens* article noted.[3]

But President Joseph Grazier described the beginning of the new decade as one of widespread disappointment for American-Standard. Sales and net income followed the construction industry's roller-coaster ride of slack demand and frenetic activity throughout the decade. Charges of antitrust violations continued and even resulted in criminal convictions for several executives.

The turbulence eventually would prompt a new, charismatic leader named Bill Eberle to move American-Standard away from reliance on the construction industry. His diversification strategy would soon fuel controversy as the company fell into heavy debt for the first time in its history.

Face-Off with the Justice Department

Grazier had vowed to battle the 1956 charge of violations of the Clayton Act, but by 1960 it was apparent that years of litigation lay ahead. Continuing to fight would not have served shareholders or the company, so the decision was made in September 1960 to get rid of the Youngstown Kitchens Division, manufacturer of sinks, cabinets and other kitchen products.

In announcing the decision, Grazier maintained that American-Standard had violated no laws:

The wall-mounted toilet was designed to make cleaning under the toilet easier.

"Our lawyers tell us it might be several more years before the case could be tried and any appeals finally determined, resulting in additional expenditures of money and executive time. I would like to emphasize that the settlement in no way interferes with our intention or ability to remain in the steel plumbing fixtures business. We are an important factor in this market, and we intend to remain so."[4]

In 1960, U.S. Attorney General William P. Rogers announced that the antitrust consent judgment required American-Standard to sell the Youngstown Division.[5]

The decision took an emotional toll, recalled David De Wahl, general counsel and corporate secretary at the time. "The decision cost the company a great deal because it made Joe Grazier timid. It weighed heavily on his entrepreneurial spirit.[6]

"The case was wrongheaded. ... American-Standard had another kitchen business and was a potential entrant on a bigger scale into the market. But the whole market was shifting to wood and away from metal, and Mullins was a steel manufacturing company."[7]

The bad news continued as it became obvious that housing starts had leveled off in 1960. The company's sales and profits that year actually declined from 1959 levels. Grazier said increased competition and decreased demand were responsible for the dip. Sales of housing products in the United States dropped from $397 million in 1959 to $353 million in 1960.[8]

Late in 1960 the company acquired Rochester Manufacturing, Inc., a maker of pressure and temperature instruments, to expand sales by acquiring new product lines. This coincided with various attempts to streamline and consolidate the growing number of divisions.

New Products for a Modern World

American-Standard joined the space race (which had begun when Sputnik I was launched October 4, 1957) by supplying an improved horizon scanner, essential for the proper orientation of satellites in 1961. The scanner's success brought more space-related contracts to the Advanced Technology Laboratories Division. This division had its beginning in 1956 when Graizer centralized the various technological research segments scattered

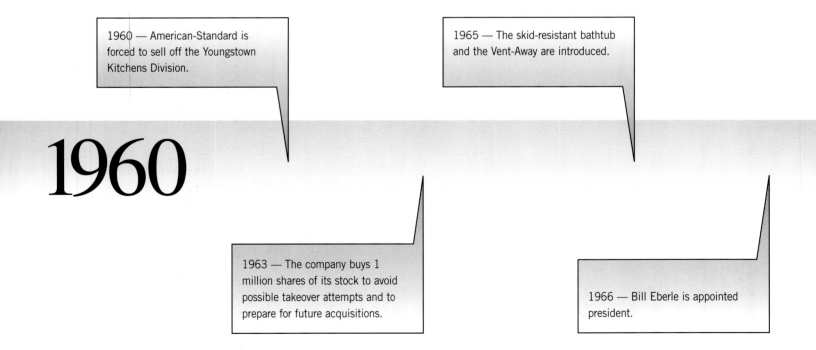

1960 — American-Standard is forced to sell off the Youngstown Kitchens Division.

1965 — The skid-resistant bathtub and the Vent-Away are introduced.

1960

1963 — The company buys 1 million shares of its stock to avoid possible takeover attempts and to prepare for future acquisitions.

1966 — Bill Eberle is appointed president.

across the company. By 1962, this particular division was supplying infrared horizon sensors for use in Project Gemini, in which astronauts competed with cosmonauts and each other in how many times they could orbit the earth.

In the area of air conditioning, the company had been working with the U.S. Army to develop a device to cool missile control vans. The units used the thermoelectric principle or "heating and cooling obtained by the passage of direct current through metallic compounds." It was thought that this could be the forerunner of more compact heating and cooling devices. American-Standard was in the process of developing an ultra-thin air conditioner, *The New York Times* reported in a front-page story:

"The new device could fit flush — or even be indented a little — in any standard wall," the article explained. "The only moving parts would be miniature fans to circulate the cooled air, and there would be no refrigeration gases."[9] The article noted that American-Standard

was "tight-lipped" about whether the product could make its way into the average consumer's home.

Though the company had embarked on research and development on many fronts, it never abandoned its hold on the bathroom.

The modern-looking "push and pull" faucet had been developed for showers, bathtubs and lavatories, and the company continued to improve its water closet design. Additionally, the company's various divisions manufactured controls for other products, including a device for dishwashers that automatically dispensed a rinse compound at the right point in the cycle. The company also developed a valve that allowed vending machines to mix a number of different hot beverages in the same machine, using a single hot water supply.

The "push and pull" faucet gave a modern look to kitchens and bathrooms.

1966 — Two executives are indicted on charges of price fixing.

1968 — Sales top $1 billion for the first time.

1969

1967 — The company plans to acquire Mosler Safe Company and Westinghouse Air Brake.

The Beginning of Diversification

In 1962 sales were up domestically and internationally, but profits for domestic operations were lower than the year before. At the annual stockholders meeting held in April 1962 at Carnegie Hall in New York, Grazier responded to a shareholder's question about whether the company should buy its stock back to perhaps purchase companies outside its core products.

Grazier was skeptical: "There's a problem of money. It takes cash and we don't want to borrow for that. Our main business is plumbing, heating and air conditioning."[10] By September 1963, however, Grazier seemed to have had a change of heart. He announced that American-Standard planned to purchase approximately 1 million shares of common stock from its shareholders at $19 per share. American-Standard anticipated it would borrow an amount "probably not exceeding $20 million from a bank or banks."[11]

"We hope that approximately 1 million shares will be offered to the company. This action is being taken in line with our program of purchasing common stock for possible future acquisitions and other business purposes," Grazier told *The New York Times*.[12]

The acquisitions were not mentioned, but Grazier was positioning the company to avoid a possible hostile takeover. The company's strong balance sheet made it "an obvious duck for a takeover raid, and the money wasn't making any money," said Fred Jaqua, former vice

president and general counsel. "So we had to get some new blood and diversify, and that's what we did."[13] The move would enable American-Standard to purchase two of its most important acquisitions that decade: Mosler Safe and Westinghouse Air Brake.

In 1963 the company entered the water supply and wastewater disposal business when it joined forces with Southern Gulf Utilities, Inc., to form Gulfstan Corporation.[14] A year later, Grazier reported welcome news: total sales reached a record-breaking $559 million. Unfortunately, profits overall remained relatively low at an unacceptable 3 percent of sales.

From Sanitation to Satellites

The company continued to expand around the world and was not shy in entering new product areas. By the end of 1965, American-Standard was operating 25 plants in 15 countries under either its own name or the Ideal Standard name. The list of products and their applications was lengthy. Plants manufactured air conditioning, furniture, heating, plumbing, refrigeration and ventilating equipment for consumer use. For industry, the company made equipment for such processes as air pollution control, heat transfer, heating, power transmission and refrigeration. American-Standard also produced parts for aircraft, space vehicles, ships and buses.

The company was proud to introduce four products in 1965, including skid-resistant bathtubs, a toilet that used the odor-removing Vent-Away system, remote control drain pop-ups for the kitchen sink and shower receptors with tile that matched the bathroom wall.[15]

Since the early years, the company had been manufacturing toilets, tubs and lavatories made of either porcelain-enameled metal or vitreous china. The latter process had always required a great deal of hand labor. But by 1965 American-Standard had managed to

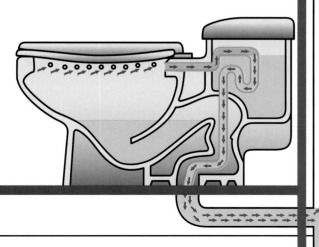

In 1968, American-Standard introduced the self-ventilating toilet.

The fresh one

A toilet that ventilates itself? This has to be the freshest idea since American-Standard moved plumbing indoors!

The remarkable new Compact/Vent-Away keeps your bathroom happily fresh always. Have it installed in about an hour, for less than $150.†

(You already have a toilet? Without Vent-Away it's like owning a car without wheels.)

The revolution is on at American-Standard.

AMERICAN STANDARD

Above: "Without Vent-Away it's like owning a car without wheels," read one of the advertisements for the Vent-Away toilet.

Right: American-Standard continued its tradition of helping consumers match colors by providing color schemes.

complete the mechanization of some of its vitreous china production processes. For example, in 1965, the glaze that is applied to fixtures before they get fired in the kiln could finally be applied automatically. Additionally, automatic molding machines and pouring furnaces were added to the plumbing fixture production processes.

"The industry was always low-tech," said Alexander Apostolopoulos, who began as plant manager of the Greek facility and rose to vice president and group executive for the Americas International Division. "But our plants became very modern within an industry that was traditionally low tech."[16]

Into New Markets

The diversification strategy went into high gear with the appointment of William D. Eberle as company president, following Grazier's election to chairman of the board in 1966. Eberle had been recruited from Boise Cascade to "pep up" the company, *Forbes* magazine reported. Boise Cascade had been considering merging with American-Standard, but the latter's poor earnings performance caused Boise to back off. Eberle, one of Boise's executive vice presidents, accepted the challenge of turning American-Standard around, however.

Eberle said the problem was that whenever home construction fell off, so did American-Standard's sales, profits and stock returns. In addition, consumer spending habits had changed.

"A john is a john is a john," Eberle told *Fortune* in the spring of 1967. "We're no longer in a 'need' society, and people will spend more for something they want. So we have to develop a total bathroom — like the General Electric kitchen — so that people won't accept just any bathroom."[17]

NEW GLAMOUR KITCHEN COLOR... AUTUMN GOLD FROM: AMERICAN-STANDARD

Complete line of kitchen appliance colors from American-Standard: new Autumn Gold, Avocado, Coppertone and appliance White.

Fiesta triple bowl kitchen sink center (P 7110, 42" x 21") and Party Sink (P 7052, 15" x 12") in new Autumn Gold

Have a Fiesta! Have it with all the brightness and warmth of sunny autumn. Have a Fiesta kitchen sink center in new AUTUMN GOLD to color-coordinate with the newest, popular appliance color for kitchens.

Now, American-Standard offers a complete line of color-harmonized kitchen appliance colors: new Autumn Gold, Avocado, Coppertone, appliance White. All available on acid-resisting enameled cast iron Fiesta, Custom-Line and Party Sinks. All designed to create the total color-coordinated kitchen. All year round!

We've captured the mellow golden warmth of Indian Summer. Bright! A ripe, rich harvest color. Warm! Like gleaming, welcome sunshine. Goes great with appliances available in this new mellow hue. Goes great with food, too. AUTUMN GOLD.

Fiesta dual-level kitchen sink center (P 7130, 32" x 21") in Avocado

Fiesta single bowl kitchen sink center (P 7150, 24" x 21") in Coppertone

AMERICAN STANDARD
PLUMBING & HEATING DIVISION

To do this, Eberle said the company would spend more on advertising and marketing, cut product lines and set up stricter controls to ascertain which products were making money. He also was not averse to borrowing. "Look at my record," he told *Fortune*. "I'm a believer in debt."[18] When he left Boise Cascade in 1966, he said, long-term debt was $193 million against capital of $192 million. In his personal finances, Eberle used debt to build an Idaho real estate empire.

Eberle's strategy created a legion of critics, then and now. But even his detractors acknowledged that his charismatic style woke the corporation up and sent it in many directions. "Bill Eberle got a great deal of public criticism in the financial press, but he really deserves credit for a major transformation of American-Standard," said David De Wahl, who served as general counsel and corporate secretary during the era.

"I once added up the acquisitions, and there were about 110 significant acquisitions. Some were only product lines, but it transformed the company from being a bathtub and boiler business into being a much broader-scale industrial enterprise."[19]

Fred Jaqua said Eberle "did some very wonderful things in a way that left us perilously poised to go bankrupt. But we certainly had changed. We had become an exciting, dynamic corporation going off in all directions."[20]

Eberle's legacy is still disputed by the executives who served under him. Herb Hadley, who was director of benefits administration, said Eberle's plan "was the right one at that time. We grew a lot, became more diversified. It was a challenging, hectic time."[21] Hugh Hoffman, head of U.S. chinaware manufacturing in 1998, said Eberle's basic goal of weaning the company from the cyclic construction industry was sound.[22]

Others disagree. Eberle "was one of those fast-racing merger and acquisition types," said John Grant, who was executive vice president and a company director at the time. "He bought anything that was there, just because it existed, not because there was any relationship with our products. He damn near put the company on the rocks."[23]

The company began to prepare for its new incarnation (today's American Standard name, without a hyphen) when it introduced a simplified trademark that was used with both the American-Standard and the overseas Ideal-Standard Name. "A modern, easy-to-read lettering style has been adopted for our two trade-names. ... As the program progresses, recognition of us as an international company serving markets throughout the world will steadily increase," Eberle announced.[24]

Back to the Courts

Eberle's acquisitions strategy may have also been influenced by yet another charge of anti-competitive practice, which resulted in jail terms for one executive, a suspended sentence for another and a series of fines for the company. Leaders throughout the plumbing fixture industry were indicted by a federal grand jury in 1966 for price fixing. A jury convicted Joseph Decker and Dan Quinn for their alleged part in price fixing. Decker went to jail for 60 days, while Quinn was given a suspended sentence.

Carl Zeigler, pricing administrator in 1998, recalled the day two "big U.S. marshals came into the office with a subpoena and said, 'Here you are. Have a nice day.'"[25] Zeigler said the company redoubled its efforts to keep pricing fair. "You've got to do it legally, no matter how nitpicky it gets. I use that always as an example — you've got to do it legally or you'll go to jail."

Whether these and other industry executives were actually engaged in price fixing is still questioned by company executives. David De Wahl knew many of the people involved.

"I don't think they ever thought of themselves as fixing prices at all. They thought they could attend trade association meetings and talk about markets with their competitors, exchanging information, without the unavoidable appearance of conspiring. People talk about the market at trade shows because that's their sole reason for being there, to exchange information."[26]

"I knew Decker and Quinn, both of whom are wonderful people," said John Donnelly, who worked on the case while a lawyer at the Sullivan Cromwell firm in New York City and eventually became general counsel for the company. "I think the jury conviction was really quite inappropriate."

"But there was enough evidence in a complex economic case that you could see how a jury could reach that conclusion. Antitrust is hard to find now in American law, but if you go back to the beginnings of the statute, the Sherman Act, you find the manufacturing industries tended to have antitrust actions brought against them every so often."[27]

TOILET TALK

SOCIAL MOVEMENTS THROUGHOUT THE 1960s toppled many traditional ideas and taboos, as people brought major issues like civil rights and the Vietnam War to the forefront of the national agenda.

One of the lesser-known issues made television history in 1968 when Phil Donahue held a frank and open discussion of toilets and bathrooms, subjects that had been shunned by television stations. Donahue was talking with a friend, William Barlow, who was general sales manager for Gibbons Supply in Dayton, Ohio. "Phil was explaining how he had been a little disappointed about the fixtures in his new home and wondered if there was 'anything new,'" related a story in the *Action Report*, an American-Standard publication. Barlow explained to Donahue some of the new products, which many people had never heard of because "TV ethics prohibited realistic plumbing explanations, and therefore we had to rely on printed media for public contact."[1]

Donahue's revolutionary talk-show format did not shy away from the controversial so long as the topic was treated with professionalism and maturity. He teamed up with Barlow and American-Standard to produce a show dedicated to the heretofore unmentionable topic of plumbing fixtures. The show's open format resulted in more than 2,000 calls, taken both during the hour-long program and days afterwards.

"Interestingly, all the calls were from women, and they spoke frankly about the toilets and bathroom facilities, as though they were calling friends instead of a television station. Some 30 questions came in during air time, ranging from why there were no seats on bidets to residential urinals for men.

"Detroit District Manager Bob Holmes said it was like one big free hour-long commercial for American-Standard. ...People still refer to the telecast, indicating it had some influence on their product selection. So the end result was an outstanding sales promotion effort, as well as a milestone in our effort to educate the consumer concerning plumbing products without offending his concept of 'good taste.'"[2]

Action Report
By and for the salespower people at American-Standard
Vol. 1, No. 3   Oct., 1968
Issued Bi-Monthly by the Communications Group Plumbing & Heating Division

Dayton TV Show Topples Toilet Taboo!

From left to right: Bob Holmes, Detroit District Manager; Phil Donahue of WLW-D TV; Bob Williams and sales rep Caryl Rader pose together after successful TV broadcast.

Interested visitors crowd around Vent-Away toilet display during Grand Opening of Gibbons Supply showroom in Dayton. A large selection of American-Standard products was exhibited.

American-Standard stood by its executives and reimbursed them for their legal fees.[28] Donnelly said the number of mergers between companies in similar industries fell off. A company seeking to grow in the late 1960s through acquisitions and mergers "picked a far-flung, distant industry that had no relationship to anything you were doing. This had the unintended consequence of driving companies to acquire things only because they knew nothing about them."[29]

The legal consideration would dovetail neatly with Eberle's plan to grow American-Standard by acquiring companies that were, necessarily or not, widely divergent from its traditions.

But until 1967, American-Standard was still primarily a plumbing and heating company. A study conducted by Cornell University provided an exhaustive review of the state of the American bathroom and found it wanting in many respects. The $100,000 report took six years to complete and was principally funded by American-Standard. Conducted under the supervision of Professor Alexander Kira, the first-of-a-kind study received widespread attention in the media and brought the discussion of the bathroom out of the closet. *The New York Times* gave front-page play to the study.

"Their conclusions range from a modest suggestion that the bathtub drain be placed at the opposite end from the faucet to facilitate cleaning to a radical redesigning of the toilet to make it lower and wider and to add a fold-down urinal for men and a bidet-like device to its equipment. ... There are hundreds of other suggestions in the report, ranging from recommendations to make the bathroom safer for children and the elderly to the provision of a place to put an ashtray."[30]

The study was mentioned in American-Standard's 1966 Annual Report as "only one of several methods we are using to pioneer in plumbing fixture design." The company's research teams also began testing the use of plastics, stainless steel, high density porcelain and lightweight metals in place of the more expensive vitreous china and enameled iron and steel.

Advances in the company's other lines continued as well, including a new line of residential furnaces equipped with solid-state controls allowing more constant room temperature; new designs and colors for modern kitchen sinks; a shock-resistant thermometer for naval use; and a boiling point indicator for heavy-engine cooling systems.[31]

A New Direction: The Mosler Acquisition

American-Standard's course changed dramatically when Eberle made the first of his major acquisitions in 1967, with the purchase of the Mosler Safe Company. "At long last, the American Radiator & Standard Sanitary Corporation may have found a merger partner that would give it insurance against seasonal and cyclical setbacks," wrote business columnist Robert Mets on May 11, 1967, in *The New York Times*.[32] The next day, American-Standard purchased 46 percent of the Mosler Safe Company stock. The stock, held by members of the Mosler family and "some key exec-

Gustav Mosler, founder of Mosler Safe.

utives and certain trusts," was sold to the company at $38.50 a share. By May 15, American-Standard had acquired 55 percent of Mosler stock and by June 2, 90.6 percent.[33]

Eberle said the company acquired Mosler as "part of our program of diversifying our business, and we are pleased to welcome the Mosler management and employees to the company."[34]

As part of American-Standard, Mosler operated as a separate division, and John Mosler, chairman of Mosler Safe, became an American-Standard director and officer. Eberle predicted that in 1967 Mosler could contribute "as much as 15 cents a share" to the company's earnings.[35] Mosler produced security systems and was involved in graphic arts, which included producing bank stationery, business forms, commercial printing and checks.

A Brief History of Mosler

When American-Standard acquired the family-owned Mosler Safe Company in 1967, it purchased a company rich in history. In business for nearly 100 years, Mosler had forged its reputation for building safes impenetrable to any assault, whether from natural calamity or human invention.

Gustav Mosler founded the company in 1848 in Cincinnati, Ohio, and left his share of the company to sons Moses and William when he died in 1874. Throughout the late 1800s and into the new century, Mosler grew and expanded the business in step with the nation's need for security systems.

Part of the secret was design innovation: in the 1880s, Mosler patented the screw-door burglary safe featuring a three-movement time lock. The design eliminated lock spindle holes, openings through which explosives could be forced. This represented a tremendous improvement over the conventional design.[36]

Under the management of the Mosler sons, in 1891 the company moved to Hamilton, Ohio. The Moslers evidently foresaw the growing need for their products and in the late 1890s decided to invest in heavy machinery for manufacturing. With this in mind, the Moslers acquired the Corliss Safe Company of Providence, Rhode Island, in 1895, taking over its manufacturing equipment and moving it to Hamilton. By the turn of the century, mirroring Standard Sanitary and American Radiator's

Mosler's safes used the same manganese steel employed in tank treads.

progress, Mosler had become the world's largest producer of its product.

During World War I, Mosler did its part in the war effort, manufacturing 55mm gun carriages. The war also spurred the demand for safe deposit boxes as patriotic citizens bought Liberty Bonds and needed a safe place to keep them. In 1918, the brothers acquired Victor Safe and Lock Company, which made manganese screw door safes, highly in demand.[37] That same year, William Mosler passed away, and in 1922, another torch passed

MOSLER SAFES VAULT OVER THE COMPETITION

MOSLER SAFES WERE SAID TO BE THE bane of thieves. In his autobiography, the infamous bank robber Willie Sutton revealed that upon breaking into a jewelry store one night, "my heart sank when I saw it was a Mosler safe. Those Mosler people certainly make safe safes."[1]

No wonder that the honor fell to Mosler to install the world's first large round vault door in New York City's then-tallest skyscraper — the Singer Sewing Machine building — in the early 1900s. Mosler commemorated the achievement by creating an advertisement depicting the Singer Building — an astounding 42 stories high — among the "Wonders of the World."[2]

Mosler was soon called upon to provide the doors for new gold storage vaults at Fort Knox, Kentucky. The doors, 21 inches thick, made of torch- and drill-resistant metals, protected more than $5 billion in gold when the facility opened in 1937.

Mosler safes even withstood the atomic blast that helped end World War II. The Teikoku Bank, Limited, of Hiroshima, Japan, sent a testimonial letter (right) to the company in 1950.

In 1960, Mosler built what was considered the world's largest vault door for the Union Carbide Company in Oak Ridge, Tennessee, which was conducting experiments with radioactive material. Fifteen feet high, the double doors were each five feet thick, with an 11-foot space in between them. Due to the precision-balanced construction, which made use of special hinges and ball bearings, one person was able to open the 250,000-pound door. As banking became more sophisticated, Mosler would transform itself with trends, entering the passcard, television surveillance, tellerless banking and pneumatic tube industries.

The Teikoku Bank, Limited
Kawayacho, Hiroshima Japan.

May 22, 1950

To the Manager
The Mosler Safe Co.
Hamilton, Ohio, U. S. A.

1950 JUN 3 AM 10:17

Sir,

We consider it our great honour to inform you that The Teikoku Bank, the successor to The Mitsui Bank, had in 1925 when it's Hiroshima branch was newly built dared to set two vault doors made by your Hamilton Factory.

As you know in 1945 the Atomic Bomb fell on Hiroshima, and the whole city was destroyed and thousands of citizens lost their precious lives. And our building, the best artistic one in Hiroshima, was also destroyed, However it was our great luck to find that though the surface of the vault doors were heavily damaged, its contents were not affected at all and the cash and important documents were perfectly saved. The superiority of your goods are completely verified as truly told to the whole world in the American Bankers, the July 13th issue of 1946. Your products were admired for being stronger than the Atomic Bomb.

Since then about five years have elapsed. The building and doors of the vault have been completely repaired and we have started our business on the first of this month. Recently many tourists from the United States and other foreign countries have come to see our building and when we show them your vault we proudly explain to them how strong they were against the Atomic explosion.

We hereby wish to have a letter of congratulations and some souvenir to celebrate our opening business at our old office. We shall appreciate it as our utmost honour, and we believe it will do much to keep and promote a good will relation for the long future.

Yours very faithfully,

The Teikoku Bank Limited

T. Yourton

Manager, Hiroshima Branch.

when Moses Mosler died and Edwin H. Mosler, Sr., became president.

After the war, more sophisticated production methods were put in place for manufacturing safes and vaults. By 1919, security equipment was in high demand among banks and businesses. Federal Reserve banks were being built, and the orders for Mosler safes started rolling in. In the mid-1920s, "Donsteel" and "Donmetal" fire- and drill-proof safes (named for Mosler sales manager J.G. Donaldson) were introduced.

Mosler entered the atomic age in 1938 and 1939 when it began manufacturing cyclotrons, also called atom smashers, in conjunction with the American Rolling Mill Company. The cyclotrons, built for the Massachusetts Institute of Technology, Ohio State University, the University of California and Westinghouse Electric, would come to play a huge part in building atomic weapons and in the reshaping of history during World War II.

Mosler also manufactured blower housings for diesel engines, condensers for escort ships, modular sections for LSTs (Landing Ship Tanks), and armor plates and turrets for Sherman tanks.

The advent of nuclear weapons following World War II brought Mosler once again to the forefront. To safeguard vital national documents like the Bill of Rights and the Declaration of Independence from nuclear blasts, Mosler built a giant "Jack-in-the-box" safe located 20 feet below the Exhibition Hall of the Archives Building in Washington, D.C. The safe could be raised to display the documents during exhibition hours, then lowered to its vault 20 feet below ground level.

Above: Mosler built the gun carriage that held the 55mm cannon on artillery pieces during World War I. The cannon itself was manufactured elsewhere.

Right: The cyclotron, a huge atom smasher, was built for universities and other organizations that conducted peacetime nuclear research in the late 1930s.

Fred Shannen, sales office manager of Los Angeles (left), is shown here presenting a Trend Setting Builder brochure to Bill Lyon, president of Lyon Homes, Inc.

In 1962, Mosler Safe went public, ending an almost 100-year run as a privately owned company. At the time, Edwin Mosler, Jr., was chairman of the board and John Mosler was president. A few years later, Edwin gave up his title to his brother John. Their brother-in-law, Martin S. Coleman, became president. William A. Marquard, who would eventually become American Standard's CEO, was named chief executive of Mosler in 1966.

Although the Mosler business flourished, relationships within the family soured. Rivalries between Martin Coleman, Edwin Mosler and John Mosler, while not publicly acknowledged, were well-known within the company. It seemed the only way to calm the waters was to sell Mosler. The owners had a unique demand, however — the acquiring party had to agree not to allow any of the family to run the company. Instead, John Mosler became a director on American-Standard's board. "This was something John Mosler insisted on," Fred Jaqua said.[38] The Mosler family also wanted cash for the company.

Future American-Standard CEO William Marquard was president of Mosler at the time of the acquisition. He said John Mosler "didn't have many opportunities to sell for cash because the family, with the kind of problems that occurred, had made up their minds that they did not want to take stock from anyone. They wanted cash, and American-Standard happened to be one of the companies that had cash."[39]

The Mosler acquisition would play a dramatic role in American-Standard's history, with implications far beyond its cash value. The Mosler purchase would bring Bill Marquard, and his connection to Kelso & Company, into American Standard's orbit — an alliance that would prove crucial in the 1980s.

Westinghouse Air Brake

While the Mosler acquisition seemed to go off without a hitch, the company's acquisition of Westinghouse Air Brake (WABCO) the following year sparked litigation that would last until the close of the decade. Based in Pittsburgh, Westinghouse Air Brake produced equipment for railroads.

Soon after the merger was announced, Crane Company — a fierce competitor of American-Standard — tried to block the deal by seeking to acquire 50 percent of Westinghouse Air Brake stock. Headquartered in New York, Crane was also a producer of plumbing fixtures. At the time, Westinghouse asserted that Crane's attempt to block the merger sprung from its desire to protect a $10 million profit it would have to give up if the merger went through.[40]

"Initially, it was a takeover battle between Crane Company and American-Standard," said Horst Hinrichs, who was chief design engineer at WABCO before the takeover and who rose to become vice chairman of American Standard's board of directors.

"American-Standard's offer was a relief because Crane didn't have a very good reputation. Nobody knew the leadership at Crane, and people were scared that everything was going to be changed. And, in hindsight, I must say that the contribution of American-Standard has been very positive."[41]

A proxy fight ensued, but on June 4, 1968, American-Standard stockholders overwhelmingly approved the plan on the same day the merger was approved by stockholders of Westinghouse Air Brake.[42] The company also prevailed in litigation launched by Crane that lasted until 1980.

Though plumbing products and air brakes seemed to have nothing in common, executives of both companies found synergies. "If you're running a company, it doesn't matter whether you're making biscuits or battleships," said G. Eric Nutter, vice president and group executive of Americas Plumbing Product Group. Nutter had worked in the Automotive Division of WABCO. "It's the principle behind it. It's leading people, letting them focus on things that really matter, the bottom line."[43]

The year 1968 was significant for another reason. That year, sales topped $1 billion. Another key merger — although not as significant as Mosler or Westinghouse — was also completed with the home building company of W.E. Lyon Development Company in Newport Beach, California. This particular merger would prove disastrous in later years, noted *Forbes* magazine in 1978.

"Eberle plunged American-Standard into California land development and expanded heating and air conditioning operations, where it took horrendous losses. What got American-Standard into trouble was simple overreaching."[44]

Project Apollo

On June 6, 1969, American-Standard acquired Melpar, Inc., a Falls Church, Virginia, company that conducted research and found applications in electronics, life sciences and other technologies.[45] The following month, Melpar helped connect the American-Standard name to the Apollo moon shot when a Melpar-designed Mobile Quarantine Facility was used to transport the Apollo crew when they returned from the lunar

American Standard dropped the hyphen from its official name in 1968, but it was still used informally in company advertisements.

mission. The quarantine room was used to prevent possible moon microbes from contaminating the earth. "Nobody had any idea what harmful material might be brought back," recalled Alan Root, then director of business planning and marketing. "We were responsible for designing an earthbound vehicular compartment into which the first returning astronauts, their spacecraft and their collection of rocks were closeted."[46]

Eberle's diversification turned American-Standard into a diversified, billion-dollar corporation. He also changed American-Standard's name to reflect its movement away from plumbing and heating. Known henceforth simply as American Standard (with the hyphen dropped), the company was no longer "American Radiator & Standard Sanitary Corporation."

Robert Crooks, who retired as chief patent counsel in 1989 after 22 years of service, said the name was changed for another reason: executives were worried that the name would become generic because "American-Standard" was simply a convenient nickname to indicate the source of products and services.[47]

American Standard entered the seventies saddled with heavy debt, more than 70,000 employees worldwide and a collection of unrelated companies in areas far afield from its original core strengths.

But though many of Eberle's acquisitions were criticized, Westinghouse Air Brake was one that stood out: "Eberle made some excellent acquisitions," conceded *Fortune* magazine. "The best of them was Westinghouse Air Brake."[48]

George Westinghouse's air brake was said to have saved more people than were killed in all wars up to World War I.

CHAPTER EIGHT

GEORGE WESTINGHOUSE AND THE AIR BRAKE

1846–1998

"His genius was never shown in brighter light than when he took up some task which other men described as impossible."

— *The New York Times*, 1914[1]

IN 1914, IT WAS SAID THAT GEORGE Westinghouse's railroad air brake had saved more lives than had been lost in all wars combined.[2]

The ability to stop a train in an emergency did not exist prior to Westinghouse's air brake, patented on April 13, 1869. Trains traveling at speeds of more than 20 miles per hour had to be braked by hand — car by car.[3] When a train engineer spotted an oncoming train or an obstacle on the tracks, he sounded the whistle to signal the train's brakemen: "The first action was to signal danger, and to this signal the train crew was instructed to respond with all celerity," explained a railroad safety book. "Each operation required time, and every second of time represented many feet of space."[4] The brakemen rushed from car to car, manually applying hand brakes in each car. An emergency often resulted in tragedy.

According to legend, Westinghouse began developing his idea for the revolutionary braking system in 1867, when his train trip from Troy to Schenectady was delayed because two freight trains had collided on the tracks ahead. Each engineer watched in horror as the other train approached, but there wasn't enough time for brakemen to stop the trains.[5]

Determined to build a better braking system, Westinghouse considered both steam and electricity as power sources but discarded them as imprac-

tical. Having read that crews used compressed air to power their rock drills as they carved the Mont Cenis tunnel through the Italian Alps, he decided to focus on that method, adapting it to fit a brake application. He reasoned that engineers had used 3,000 feet of pipeline — a distance far longer than any train — to pump the air into the mountain to power their rock drills, and "a rock drill moved by air compressed to one-sixth its natural bulk and, consequently, when set free, exercising an expansive force equal to six atmospheres,"[6] noted an account of the drilling. The young inventor shrugged off the derision of those who said he was "trying to stop the movement of a train ... with wind!"[7] and set to work on his air brake, a project that would take two years to complete but one that would revolutionize the railroad industry.

With the financial support of a Pittsburgh foundry executive, 23-year-old George Westinghouse was able to build and demonstrate a prototype. In September 1868, when he had perfected it, the young inventor equipped a five-car train, bound from Pittsburgh, Pennsylvania, to Steubenville, Ohio, with his new device.

Wheel brakes on an early automobile in France.

As the train emerged from a tunnel, chugging along at a steady 30 miles an hour, the engineer "was horrified to see a huckster's cart on the tracks two city blocks away," according to a railroad history. "The driver applied his whip. The horses reared upright and stalled the cart directly in the path of the approaching train. "Without much faith," the conductor pulled the strange brake handle.[8] The train stopped four feet short of the cart. "Everyone, especially the carriage driver, looked upon it as a miracle," noted a history of Westinghouse Air Brake.[9] Westinghouse had just accomplished the first emergency stop in railroad history. He was convinced that his new invention would enjoy wide appeal so he founded Westinghouse Air Brake Company, which was shortened to just WABCO in later years. Manufacturing operations began the following year, 1870, at Liberty and 25th Street in Pittsburgh.

The first successful emergency stop using Westinghouse's air brake was depicted in a book commemorating the company's 75th anniversary, celebrated in 1944.

1846 — George Westinghouse is born.

1869 — Westinghouse Air Brake Company is founded.

1846

1868 — The air brake is successfully demonstrated and patented the following year.

1881 — Westinghouse expands into Europe.

The air brake worked by piping compressed air from the locomotive's steam-driven air compressor through a complicated piping system that eventually led to the brake shoes of each train car. The locomotive engineer had complete control of the system and could apply the brakes whenever he wanted. No longer was valuable time wasted in the signaling of brakemen.[10]

A Fertile Mind

Born on October 6, 1846, in the village of Central Bridge, New York, Westinghouse was destined to become one of America's most prolific inventors. Chief among his contributions to science and society were the implementation in the United States of the alternating electric current system for readily available power; the use of natural gas for domestic and industrial fuel; and a device that replaced derailed cars on the tracks simply and easily, his first patented invention.[11]

When he was a boy, his father moved the family to Schenectady, New York, where the young George Westinghouse spent all his free time tinkering with machinery and learning how it worked. While still a young teenager,

Westinghouse designed and constructed his own rotary steam engine. Upon the outbreak of the Civil War, he enlisted in the Union army. At first Westinghouse joined a cavalry regiment, but soon his superiors discovered his aptitude for engineering and he was transferred to the Navy, where he served in the engineer corps as a third assistant engineer until 1865.

After the war, Westinghouse entered Union College. Although he excelled at mathematics, a professor counseled that the university was only holding him back, and Westinghouse left school to pursue his destiny of becoming an engineer and an inventor.[12]

Among his many inventions, Westinghouse developed a system of automatic signals, powered by compressed air, to tell engineers when to stop the trains. In an unrelated field, and years ahead of his time, Westinghouse invented an automatic telephone exchange system. Perhaps the infant communications industry was not ready for such an invention because although it worked, the system was never put into use while Westinghouse was alive. Those in the industry at the time did not believe the phone system could function without switchboard operators.[13]

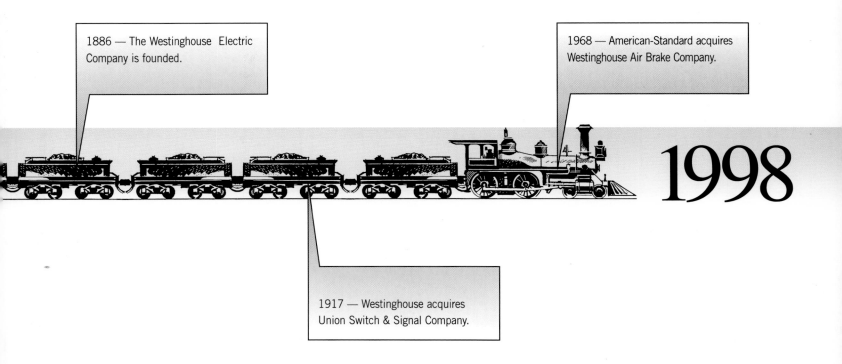

1886 — The Westinghouse Electric Company is founded.

1968 — American-Standard acquires Westinghouse Air Brake Company.

1998

1917 — Westinghouse acquires Union Switch & Signal Company.

In the late 1880s, Westinghouse became interested in a device called an alternating current motor. In Westinghouse's day, direct or continuous current could only be transmitted short distances from a generator. In Europe, Westinghouse learned, a machine had been invented to make use of alternating current, but it had not reached the United States. Westinghouse, having founded the Westinghouse Electric Company in 1886, bought the patents and lobbied for the use of alternating current in the United States. Controversy surrounded the alternating current system, however, and it wasn't until June 1912 that he received the Edison Gold Medal for his contribution to the alternating current system.[14]

Westinghouse was described as a big man with a heart to match his intellect and bearing. He rarely lost control of his temper, and it was said that he had the gift of being able to inspire those who worked with and around him. His career flourished until a financial panic in 1907 weakened his support with his board of directors. He was eased out and became estranged from his former associates, and his health suffered.[15] When he died on March 12, 1914, at the age of 68, he owned between 35 and 40 companies capitalized at $200 million and employing 50,000.[16]

Westinghouse garnered many honors in his lifetime. Union College, from which he had dropped out many years before, bestowed an honorary doctorate in philosophy and various other honorary degrees upon him. France enrolled him in the Legion of Honor; he was the second recipient of the John Fritz Medal awarded by leading U.S. engineering societies and the first American to receive the Grashoff Medal, awarded by the Association of German Engineers. In 1957, a bust of George Westinghouse was unveiled in the Hall of Fame of Great Americans in New York City.[17]

"Intentionally or otherwise," declared a letter to the editor of *The New York Times*, "he made himself a benefactor of the race."[18]

The Air Brake

In the year the air brake was first demonstrated, there were 40,000 miles of track in the United States. Not only did the air brake have a major influence on train travel safety, it also had an influence on the growth of railroads. Between 1870 and 1880 the miles of track doubled in the United States, and in the following decade that number doubled again.[19] Still, the use of the air brake did not catch on as quickly as some in the railroad industry would have liked.

Pullman, the famous maker of railroad cars, was among the first companies to endorse the new air brake. However, since the company made only cars and not the locomotives themselves, Pullman did not wield the kind of influence that could have led to wider use of the air brake from the outset. One common complaint about the new type of brake was that it was "so wonderfully clever that those who had to use it could not understand it."[20]

Fig. 1

But self-made railroad man John H. Devereaux lobbied for the use of the air brake even though it would be an expensive undertaking. "We can rely upon it with relief that only can be known to those who are responsible for human life and property," Devereaux wrote.[21] By 1871, many Western railways used the air brake, but trains in the East were still not equipped with Westinghouse's invention. It took a disaster on August 26, 1871, in Revere, Massachusetts, to change public opinion. Twenty-four passengers were killed by that train wreck, and finally the conservative managers of the Eastern railroads began to see the air brake as a necessity.[22]

Other lines followed Pennsylvania Railroad's lead, and within five years of Westinghouse's 1868 demonstration, 2,281 locomotives and 7,254 cars had been equipped with air brakes. A Belgian railway purchased the air brake in 1872, and a Mexican line installed the Westinghouse brake system in 1873. Soon after, France made the air brake standard equipment on all passenger cars in the country.[23] The first foreign air brake company was organized in Sevran, France, in 1879. A major expansion occurred in 1891 with the purchase of five hectares of land by Westinghouse Air Brake. (The area in Sevran where the plant was built became known as "Freinville," or, in English, "Brakeville," near Paris.)

In 1881, Westinghouse Air Brake was formed in England, followed by a company in Hanover, Germany, in 1884. Expansion around the world in later decades reached Russia, Canada, Italy,

Above: Drilling the Mont Cenis tunnel with compressed air.

Below: An early drawing of a Westinghouse-equipped Atmospheric Brake.

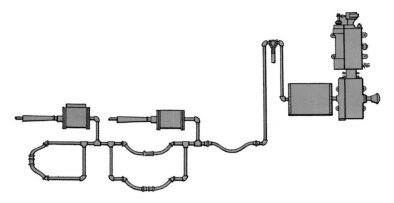

Australia, Japan, Belgium, Spain, Switzerland and Turkey.

By 1890, despite the fact that the company had moved to larger quarters in Allegheny, Pennsylvania (now part of Pittsburgh), demand for the air brake was growing too rapidly for the plant to accommodate. And so, that year, Westinghouse Air Brake Company moved to Wilmerding, Pennsylvania.

Although the air brake had proven itself, the abrupt stops it provided were not particularly smooth. The triple valve was one of the first major improvements to the air brake. In the past, the engineer had to let air into the pipeline before the train could stop. With the improvement, he let air out of the pipe, and the reduced pressure activated the triple valves automatically, making for smoother stops. The triple valve also allowed "automatic application" of the brakes in the event

that "compressed air supply was severed by, for example, a broken coupling between train cars."[24] In other words, runaway cars would stop automatically if severed from the train. Or, if the train were severed, both parts would stop because the triple valve would hold a reservoir of compressed air in each car.

In 1893, Congress passed the Federal Safety Appliance Act, which required that power brakes be used on railroad rolling stock. The following year, Westinghouse Air Brake introduced the high-speed passenger-car brake — an improved form of its earlier air brake — known as the Quick-Action Brake. The brake reduced the time it took to reduce air pressure through the train pipe, allowed for smoother stops and prevented cars farther down along the train from bumping the cars before them that had already been stopped.

As his equipment met with wider acceptance, Westinghouse saw the advantages of making each piece standard so that it could be fitted to train cars manufactured both in the United States and in Europe. Older applications could also be easily upgraded. "He thus became one of the first to adopt a modern practice of standardization," one biographer wrote.[25]

In 1901 air brakes for electric railways, with motor-driven air compressors, were introduced, followed by magnetic brakes for electric street railway cars in 1902. "All improvements in the air brake have been designed with the same fixed purpose: to make possible longer and longer trains moving more frequently with heavier loads at higher speeds, to do this with ever-increasing safety," a company publication said.[26]

The prolific inventor continued to improve and refine his creations. It is estimated that Westinghouse was awarded a new patent every six weeks for 48 years.[27] In 1908, he introduced

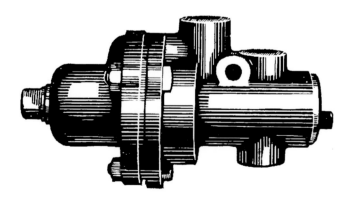

Top: The Westinghouse Straight Air Brake from 1869.

Above: The triple valve design allowed for smoother stops.

Right: The Quick-Action Brake prevented cars from bumping into each other as they stopped.

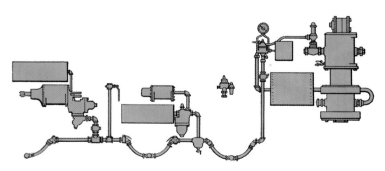

electro-pneumatic brakes for subways; in 1910 organized Westinghouse Pacific Coast Brake Company; and in 1911 began a paid vacation system for veteran employees.

George Westinghouse was known as a fair and compassionate employer. The Westinghouse Electric Company, from its founding, offered fair salary and generous benefits. Appreciative of his workers' loyalty, Westinghouse made a pioneering step toward a five-day work week (unheard of in the late 1880s) when he introduced a "free Saturday afternoon." Before his death in 1914, he established a pension plan for his employees.

Recognizing the tremendous contributions Westinghouse had made, the Franklin Institute Museum in Philadelphia opened a permanent air brake exhibit in 1939. Two years later the Smithsonian in Washington, D.C., would do the same.

Union Switch & Signal Company

In 1917, Westinghouse Air Brake acquired Union Switch & Signal Company, which had developed various systems of signaling trains and coordinating train routes. By the 1940s, some of those systems had grown quite sophisticated. For example, automatic block signaling ensured engineers kept safe distances between trains on the same track. Union Switch & Signal Company also pioneered a centralized traffic control system that used a traffic control board indicating the location of trains in certain territories, akin to modern-day radar air traffic controls. The system allowed railroads to coordinate safe routes.

Entry into the Automotive Industry

In 1921, Westinghouse developed pneumatic brakes for the small but rapidly expanding automotive industry in the United States. Under the Federal Aid Road Act of 1916, the federal government had committed more than $75 million to the construction of roads. The money was used to connect almost every town and city with a population of 5,000 or more. By the late 1920s, more than half a million miles of surfaced roads covered the United States.

Roads by now competed with rail as a mover of people and goods, and it was an obvious move

Above and below: Westinghouse's brake was adapted from trains to automobiles. The brake cylinder on this Westinghouse truck, above, and this early French fire truck, below, used the air brake system.

Left: Westinghouse built a traveling school and laboratory aboard a train. It traveled more than a million miles.

Below: Westinghouse's headquarters for the German subsidiary, located in Hanover, pictured here in 1900.

for WABCO to adapt the air brake components (compressors, valves and controls, for example) for commercial vehicles. But U.S. antitrust laws compelled WABCO to form a joint venture with Bendix rather than launch its own line of braking components. The joint venture was called Bendix-Westinghouse Automotive Air Brake Company, and its mission was to develop and sell products for cars, trucks and buses. WABCO owned 49 percent interest in the venture, with the other 51 percent of shares held by Bendix, which had been founded in 1924 to serve the automotive industry. Bendix had

introduced the Bendix Starter Drive, which eliminated the balky and often recalcitrant hand-crank starter on cars.

In Europe, where antitrust laws were less stringent, WABCO competed directly in the automotive sector as well as in the railway braking market. Except for certain financial matters and several cross-licensing agreements with Bendix-

Pneumatic controls gave a ship's captain instant command over engines and propellers.

Westinghouse, the various international companies that comprised WABCO-Europe were allowed to develop independently with little oversight from the main headquarters in the United States.

Progress in the Midst of War

Following the United States' entry into World War II, WABCO indirectly benefited as its products came into wider use. During the war, it filled its share of war production contracts, manufacturing airplane propellers, automatic pistols, carbines, aircraft bombs, high explosives and electronic devices. Its AB-1-B brake was put to frequent use. An occasional freight car equipped with the brake and packed with emergency equipment could safely be attached to a passenger train for last-minute, emergency transport.

Westinghouse had begun its research and development with pneumatics decades before World War II. After Pearl Harbor, marine engineers were looking for new ways to quickly, efficiently and safely change the direction of a marine vessel. Engineers at the Wilmerding, Pennsylvania, plant were able to fill the order. A pneumatic control was developed that could reverse a ship's direction in seconds, giving the vessel the ability to escape torpedoes, mines and bombs. It also allowed complete control of the vessel from the bridge, cutting lag time by 90 percent. Like early locomotives, orders for a change in direction were issued by the bridge to those below on the engine crew. The system of changing direction was made synchronized and automatic with pneumatics. During the war, pneumatic controls were also used aboard ship for controlling steering and flanking rudders and for operating fire pumps and giant searchlights.

Other domestic progress made during the war included improved brake equipment for diesel electric locomotives. By 1943, approximately 890,000 freight cars in the United States had been equipped with AB brakes, and by 1945, 2.16 million inter-

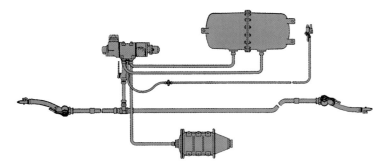

change railroad cars were equipped with the device. Advances in centralized traffic control allowed more trains to traverse the same tracks safely; train capacity had increased by 50 to 80 percent by the end of the war, though no new tracks had been laid.

Westinghouse air compressors had become standard equipment at thousands of service stations throughout the United States, and the devices were also used on oil field equipment such as cranes and steam shovels. Pneumatic controls were also giving pilots of river tow boats increased control of their vessels.

As WABCO entered the 1950s, research and development remained in the forefront of operations as the company worked to improve existing products and develop new ones.[28]

WABCO developed a new air brake control stand and improved its locomotive pneumatic throttle control equipment; several new air compressor models were also introduced for diesel locomotive designs.

The company also implemented an expansion program at the start of the decade. WABCO acquired Melpar, Inc., a company that performed electronics research and development for the U.S. armed forces, in 1951. In 1953, WABCO acquired the earth-moving business of R.G. LeTourneau, Inc., and created the wholly owned subsidiary LeTourneau-Westinghouse. At about the same time, the COBRA Shoe was developed by the Air Brake Division and Johns-Manville Corporation. The improved brake shoe was smoother, quieter, more efficient and longer lasting. Meanwhile, LeTourneau-Westinghouse was busy marketing its new two-wheel tractor with a rear dump-hauling and earth-moving scraper.

In 1952 WABCO acquired the Le Roi Company of Wisconsin, which manufactured high-quality air compressors, internal combustion engines and pneumatic tools for the oil, mining and road building industries.

The electronic train yard, an outgrowth of research conducted during the Korean War, was fully implemented during 1955. The system helped sort freight cars according to their destinations as they worked their way through a maze of tracks in the nation's busy freight yards.

"Electronic relays automatically line up switches; radar gauges the car's speed; a computer, fed data on wind resistance and track curvature, figures the proper speed for the safety of the car's cargo and automatic retarders pinch the car's wheels to control speed. The car finally bumps gently onto the proper train while behind it, other cars are moving automatically to their proper tracks at a four-a-minute rate."[29]

Above: The AB brake allowed freight trains to move as fast as passenger trains.

Below: The traveling school for railway technicians.

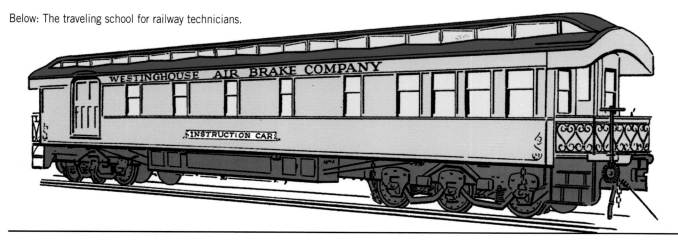

"These yards pay for themselves in a couple of years, and that's a conservative estimate," a Union Switch & Signal Division official told *The New York Times*. "The main bottleneck on railroads as they operate today is in their yard operations. The automated freight classification yard eliminates this bottleneck." At the time, Westinghouse was a major supplier of equipment to update the facilities. Typically, railroads paid anywhere from $5 million to $15 million to build electronic classification yards.[30]

The company pioneered a brave new concept — engineerless trains, the precursor of modern computerized shuttle systems. In December 1955, Union Switch & Signal set up a demonstration with the New Haven Railroad that took 75 people on a remote-controlled train ride from Larchmont to Rye, both in the state of New York. Train officials and members of the press took the 10-mile trip in a single-coach train to observe how electronic controls could successfully guide the locomotive.[31]

That same year, Melpar, Inc., developed a radar device that allowed airports to instantly identify commercial aircraft from 200 miles away. It was the precursor to a sophisticated air traffic control system that would enable traffic controllers to simultaneously sort out hundreds of aircraft in the same stretch of sky.[32]

By 1959, Union Switch & Signal was testing its system for implementing completely automatic trains for subways, company official W.A. Robinson told *The New York Times*. Though the automatic trains had yet to be installed, the company had perfected automatic controls for them.[33]

Unfortunately, the 1960s were not as profitable for WABCO as the previous decade had been. Sales in 1960 were $186 million, down 11 percent from the 1959 total of $209 million. Still, the company and its subsidiaries persevered with research and new product development. Innovations during the 1960s included an improved WABCOPAC brake assembly for freight cars, improved COBRA brake shoes and the ABD brake valve, an improved version of the AB valve.

In Europe, where WABCO was a major presence, engineers at the Turin, Italy, plant got an assignment that puzzled them, but over which they eventually triumphed.

"It had nothing to do with signaling, which is a purely railway business," said Giancarlo Aimetti, who joined WABCO in 1963 as a young engineer and rose to be group vice president for the WABCO Austrian Group.

"One day, the chief of the Italian road police came to visit us and said, 'Gentlemen, I want you to make a very special tool. I would like to know

WABCO and Teldix, of Heidelberg, Germany, cooperated to develop electronic braking systems. A competitor bought Teldix, however, and WABCO was on its own.

Official opening of a new test track in Germany (above) by (left to right) Emmanuel Kampouris, Erich Reinecke and Horst Hinrichs.

exactly — every moment — where all of my motorcycles, all of my patrol cars and all of my helicopters are, and I want to know each unit by number, and exactly which street they are on, for my whole territory.' Well, this could be a very good chance for the company, we realized. We told him this might be something we could do, and we sat down to figure out how to do it."[34]

In the mid-1960s, before the advent of the microchip, circuitry for such a system was cumbersome and expensive, but the engineers set about designing it anyway, Aimetti said.

"I did not return to my home for 26 days. We worked very, very hard, sometimes on 48-hour shifts, to manufacture the system, even though we were pretty sure we wouldn't make money on it. The police chief wanted to make a demonstration, but we had many problems with the system, and as the deadline approached, we couldn't get it to work. So we stepped up our efforts, working many hours, and we had the system working when the police chief came. The next day, our little company was on the front page of every newspaper in Italy!"[35]

The system required a great deal of maintenance, however, and was never adopted for general use, but creating it was "absolutely exciting," Aimetti said. "A key point of this company, and our customers realize it, is that we are different. We are willing to be their partner, not just their supplier."

In 1966, sales rebounded to a record total of $309 million. By 1967 the company was operating 14 plants in 11 states and one in Canada, employed 16,000 and produced 33 product lines sold to approximately 30,000 customers in 115 countries. WABCO products had become so pervasive in Europe that when American Standard finalized the acquisition of WABCO in 1969, it kept the $45 million automotive business.

In the United States, however, American Standard executives decided to sell the company's minority interest in the Bendix-Westinghouse joint venture, which appeared to serve a relatively minor market compared with American Standard's other endeavors, and keep WABCO's railway braking business along with the other product lines acquired through the years.

The acquisition by American Standard had an immediate beneficial effect for WABCO, which had grown at its own pace. WABCO's European subsidiaries were operating autonomously from a business standpoint when American Standard stepped in. They often competed with each other and had no standardized ideas, procedures, components or systems. This was true throughout Europe, where companies followed their own diagrams and safety regulations. Between a truck and a trailer in Germany, for instance, only one brake pipe was required. In France, two were required while three were mandated in Great Britain.[36]

After the acquisition, WABCO executives standardized technical details among WABCO subsidiaries and helped develop common regulations for the European Community. As Europe adopted common technical requirements, other nations around the world, such as Japan and Brazil, followed.

The movement towards standardization was a critical phase for Europe and WABCO because it prepared the way for a revolution in automotive safety, known as the antilock braking system or ABS. In 1981, WABCO pioneered the concept, building on experience gained from more than a decade of effort. While WABCO would eventually corner the ABS commercial vehicle market in Europe, its entry into the market was rocky, said Erich Reinecke, WABCO vice president of group engineering. WABCO, lacking the electronic expertise, cooperated with Teldix of Heidelberg, Germany. Finally, Bosch, WABCO's major competitor, bought Teldix, effectively taking away WABCO's capability to make ABS brakes, Reinecke said in a 1998 interview.

Bosch had offered to sign a cooperation agreement with WABCO, but Reinecke opposed it. "There was a lot of discussion here internally. Can we reach the goal of making the brakes by ourselves, or should we take the agreement that a competitor, Bosch, had offered us? We decided to reject that." WABCO eventually found a partner in Mercedes-Benz as its first major ABS customer and went on to conquer the European market.[37]

Throughout its history, WABCO has preserved the spirit of innovation. "We spend 5 to 6 percent of every sales dollar each year on product development," said Horst Hinrichs, who was chief design engineer at WABCO before it was acquired and rose to become vice chairman of American Standard's board of directors. "We're designing very, very technically driven things. We're spending $50 million per year, and you can't afford that unless you have a strong substance behind it in terms of sales."[38]

The brake company would continue to grow along with its parent, and in the late 1990s WABCO remained a major part of American Standard's business. Though the railway brake and signal business would eventually be sold off, American Standard would retain the truck and automobile brake business, which continues as a major profit center.

WABCO and American Standard strive for continuous improvement, Aimetti said. "They're always setting some sort of target, and the target is such that you're completely engaged in meeting it. Frankly speaking, that's the only way."[39]

The Radiator Building was refurbished in the seventies. The same could be said for American-Standard.

CHAPTER NINE

BACK TO BASICS

1970–1979

"I had made up my mind that there needed to be a change, and about the same time a couple of the board members came to see me one evening to suggest that they might want to make me president. If they hadn't come to me, I would have probably suggested it myself."

— William A. Marquard, 1998[1]

WESTINGHOUSE AIR BRAKE would prove one of President Bill Eberle's lasting achievements, but most of his other acquisitions would have to be jettisoned to save the 60,000-employee company from bankruptcy. Debt had rocketed from just $21 million in 1966 to $426 million in 1971, at a time when interest rates were climbing.[2]

Profits plummeted from $35 million in 1969 to $18 million one year later, and as a result the company had to report to a banking committee which had been organized to oversee American Standard's complicated and grim finances.[3]

"We just couldn't digest it all," said Sandy McGregor, who was part of American Standard's legal department at the time. "We had just acquired too much."[4] The problem was not unique to American Standard. In the sixties, many large corporations operated with the belief that a good manager could handle just about any acquisition in any industry, and they bought companies that often simply piqued a president's interest.

John Grant, an executive vice president under Eberle, resigned in 1970 because of Eberle's management style and policies but returned when William Marquard was elected president and chief executive officer. "Bill Eberle bought companies just because they existed. He was an incorrigible acquisitionist," Grant said in 1998.[5]

Saving the company fell to Marquard, Grant and another senior executive, Alan Root.

William Marquard

Marquard was clearly the man for the job, observers noted. "Mr. Marquard was totally dedicated. American Standard meant everything to him," recalled Barbara Glenn, who was his assistant at the time.[6]

Marquard was one of the most valuable assets that came along with Eberle's Mosler Safe acquisition in 1967. Born on March 6, 1920, Marquard attended grade and high school in Pittsburgh, Pennsylvania, and graduated from the Wharton School of the University of Pennsylvania. He worked for Westinghouse Electric Company (a totally separate company from Westinghouse Air Brake) before going to work for Mosler Safe in 1952.

Marquard became president of Mosler shortly after its purchase and moved into American Standard's management in 1970 as chief operating officer to help sort out the corporation's financial problems. Marquard, who was not a member of the board of directors at that point, knew he

---

The Dualux faucet sold well in Europe when it was introduced in the late 1970s.

faced a struggle to bring sense to American Standard's finances because he was not as well known to the directors as Bill Eberle.

It wasn't long before Marquard clashed with Eberle's autocratic management style, he said. "As COO I realized the depth of the problems because I had responsibility for the whole corporation from an operating standpoint."

"I became alarmed at our need for capital to support all of our diverse businesses. At that point there was disagreement between myself and Bill Eberle to the extent of how much capital was required, my feelings being that the number was much greater than what he thought it had to be. I had made up my mind that there needed to be a change, and about the same time a couple of the board members came to see me one evening to suggest that they might want to make me president. If they hadn't come to me, I would have probably suggested it myself."[7]

The decision came as a surprise to Eberle, who continued to argue with Marquard about how much capital was needed to operate the company. "But with the banks putting the pressure on, it became obvious something was going to happen," Marquard said. He assumed the reins of the company as president that same year, and Eberle became chairman until 1971, when he resigned. President Richard Nixon appointed Eberle to the international Organization for Economic Cooperation and Development. Meeting in Paris, the group was charged with making recommendations to aid international trade negotiations and foreign investment.[8]

Marquard knew that the quickest way to obtain capital was to sell off parts of the company that had become too leveraged. His first move was to sell off American Standard's land-and-housing subsidiary, W.E. Lyon Development Company, a disastrous acquisition that had been purchased in 1968. "The real estate business was a major headache to the company," said John Geer, who was general counsel at the time. "Not only was it hard to make profitable, but there were a lot of hidden liabilities in selling properties to individual home buyers. The company was happy to be rid of those businesses."[9]

Staying the Course

Marquard also installed the discipline that Grant and others said was lacking. The compa-

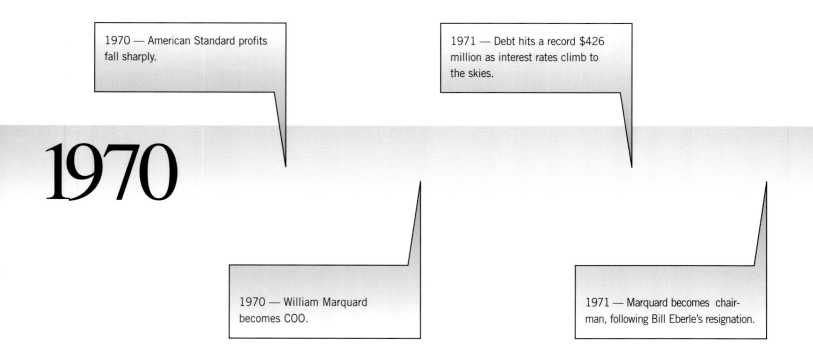

1970 — American Standard profits fall sharply.

1971 — Debt hits a record $426 million as interest rates climb to the skies.

1970

1970 — William Marquard becomes COO.

1971 — Marquard becomes chairman, following Bill Eberle's resignation.

ny's major divisions were realigned to centralize control. Plants were closed and consolidated. Aerospace and government-related contracts were phased out, and most of the assets and operations of Melpar were sold. The company made personnel cutbacks at every level, reined in capital expenditures and set new guidelines for inventory control.

"We devised a plan of what we were going to divest, and I think one of the things that was so important in getting the job done was that I insisted we never look back," Marquard later said. "There were times when we sold a business, and six months later, someone would say, 'Oh, God, we shouldn't have sold that,' but I wouldn't let anybody change their mind."[10]

The company quickly sold off the Drilling Equipment Division, the Environmental Comfort Systems Group and the Pneumatic Equipment Division, bringing in $57 million to reduce the debt in 1971.

Selling off other portions of the company was difficult because high debt made them unattractive to buyers. About 30 buildings, for instance, had second mortgages taken out by the company to try to take advantage of the prime rate.[11]

Marquard, John Grant and Alan Root devised a divestiture strategy for the troubled subsidiaries. Root recalled that for the first six months they had to "figure out what we had, and then we had to make them work better."[12]

The three men worked weekends and nights to come up with a plan to refocus the company without simply writing off unprofitable areas and taking a loss, recalled Angela Tripodi, an executive secretary for Alan Root. "I remember the way they put in long hours going over all the different businesses. They didn't just say, 'OK, we're getting rid of this.' They did very in-depth studies."[13]

But many areas of the company were not performing well. The security systems and graphic arts portion, which accounted for $193 million in 1971, suffered from virtually all facets of the slowing national economy: a leveling off in commercial construction, a downturn in government spending for defense-oriented security products, general business cost-reduction programs, and high but obsolete inventory. This particular group had once contributed 39 percent of the total income, but that figure fell to just 16 percent by 1971. Portions of the transportation systems group, which included Westinghouse Air Brake, suffered

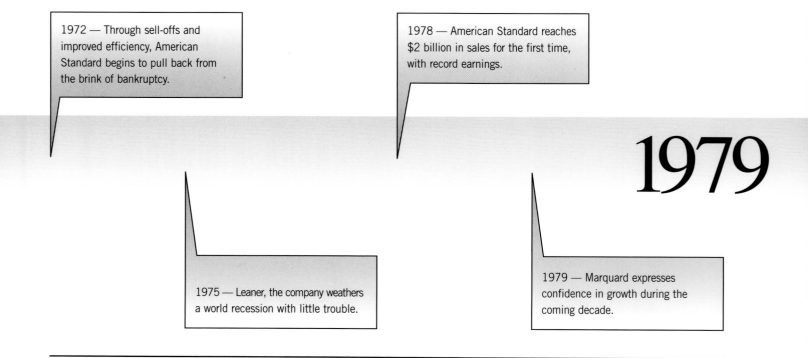

1972 — Through sell-offs and improved efficiency, American Standard begins to pull back from the brink of bankruptcy.

1978 — American Standard reaches $2 billion in sales for the first time, with record earnings.

1979

1975 — Leaner, the company weathers a world recession with little trouble.

1979 — Marquard expresses confidence in growth during the coming decade.

as well because debt-laden cities (New York City being the most infamous during this period) were forced to put off investments in their mass-transit systems.

"The period of Mr. Marquard was a very interesting and challenging one," said Hans Zinzow, who joined Westinghouse Air Brake Company in 1958 as a controller and retired from American Standard in 1989. "We had to get back to basics and become a money-earning operation piece-by-piece."[14]

In the 1971 Annual Report, Marquard outlined the strategy for identifying which businesses ought to be sold off.

"Those that are peripheral to our main lines of endeavor; those that require more additional capital than we deem it advisable to invest; or those that do not have the future profit potential to warrant the existing investment."[15]

Marquard also brought a very different management style, noted former executive vice president Robert Levinson, one of the founders of Steelcraft, which he and his brother, Charles, sold to American Standard a few years earlier. Levinson, who left the division in 1979, said Marquard delegated responsibility and authority to his group vice presidents with the insistence that they operate with good business sense: "What Marquard did is make sure his group vice presidents were good business people. He delegated the responsibility for our divisions to each of us, and he insisted on us operating those divisions on a very good, businesslike basis" as long as it was profitable.

"I had 14 companies in my division, and one of my first tasks was to try to get these companies to at least a break-even point, so I worked for a few years to try to do that and then I began to dispose of those companies. We all worked hard, and we pulled the company through."[16]

Executives decided to restructure American Standard's tax portfolio, as well. "Tax was always very important," said Henry Steiner, who was tax counsel. "I started restructuring American Standard's foreign subsidiaries in a more tax-effective way beginning with Canada and

William Marquard, at the 1971 annual stockholders meeting. Immediately next to Marquard is Bill Eberle, who was still chairman when this photo was taken. David De Wahl, general counsel at the time, is on Eberle's right.

then throughout Europe, Mexico, Central and South America."

"I typically combined different subsidiaries which were serving the purposes of different business divisions, combining them into a single corporate identity in order to have losses and profits offset each other, and to provide for easier cash transfers among the divisions without a tax cost."[17]

The end of 1971 saw some improvement, with earnings rising to $33.2 million, though the company still lost $83 million from the restructuring plan. In many areas, American Standard had deliberately restricted sales volume to reduce overhead cost and funds tied up in working capital.

The company was still the leader in many fields, including its core strength — plumbing. That same year, American Standard secured a $9 million plumbing contract for the World Trade Center in New York City. When completed, the famous twin towers contained 10,000 colored American Standard plumbing fixtures, including 2,600 toilets, 2,274 lavatories and 1,000 urinals.

Two years later American Standard broke another record when it won the largest plumbing contract in Nevada history at the famed MGM Grand Hotel. The $106 million hotel, which opened in 1974, was lavishly equipped with American Standard plumbing fixtures. In deluxe rooms like the Rhett Butler suite, such elegant products as the Ultra tub, Carlyle closets, Ovalyn lavatories, Margate bidets and Heritage brass faucets with acrylic handles were installed.

Silver Linings

The austerity program cut American Standard's debt from $425.7 million to $312 million by the end of 1972 with an improvement in earnings as well.[18] By then, all cast-iron sanitary fixture production had been consolidated at the Louisville plant, and more cost-effective materials such as plastics were being used in greater quantities for bathtubs.

The Mosler Division was seeing success with its Remote Transaction System and the Mosler Teller-Matic or "push-button" banking machine. The first system used television screens and pneumatic

American Standard battled back from near-bankruptcy, helped by an increase in housing starts in 1977. Here, a worker applies enamel to a red-hot bathtub.

tubes. Customers could walk up and make their transactions while communicating with a teller on the screen. The idea behind the system was to protect tellers and their cash drawers from bank robbers. The Mosler Teller-Matic was basically a forerunner of the modern ATM machine, which was just moving out of the prototype stage in 1972. The Westinghouse Air Brake Division experienced a sales slowdown in 1972 because freight car construction in the United States was at its lowest level since 1963, but Westinghouse rebounded the following year, when domestic freight car production experienced an increase and truck production picked up in Europe.

Other American Standard lines experienced the same kind of high demand. Banks were growing, adding branches that created demand for Mosler banking products. Meanwhile, domestic mining operations were on the upswing, creating a demand for off-highway trucks.[19] Though building products comprised almost half of the company's sales in 1973, strikes at domestic vitreous china plumbing fixture and steel door plants

Above and inset: Almost all segments of American Standard improved, including WABCO, which was producing trucks for a growing European market.

caused this division to be the least profitable. The 57 percent increase in overall corporate earnings (which had returned to $39.5 million) came primarily from transportation, security systems, construction and mining operations.[20]

Mosler continued to innovate products in the still-strong security market when it introduced a new card-activated security system called Accessor. The system permitted authorized personnel to walk through a door only if they had a special magnetically coded ID card.[21] That same year, the New York & Suburban Federal Savings and Loan office on Manhattan's Upper West Side introduced one of Mosler's Remote Transaction or "tellerless banking" systems.

Eventually, however, the decision was made to sell off the Electronic Transaction Division.

"Mosler had gotten off to a late start," said Roy Satchell, who retired in 1985 as senior vice president of security and graphics. "The market at the time was already dominated by Diebold and IBM. We decided we didn't have the time or the technology to turn what was basically a metal bending business into a high-tech company, so we sold that division to TRW."[22]

In 1973 the global economy shuddered when OPEC embargoed oil, the lifeblood of the industrialized world, to nations that supported Israel during the Yom Kippur War. Inflation hit 12 percent, prompting economists to coin the term "stagflation" to describe the twin malaise of inflation and recession.

A leaner American Standard weathered these shocks much better than many companies during this time, and continued to make progress towards refocusing itself and paying down its debt. By the end of 1974, the company had gotten rid of the Mutschler kitchen cabinet opera-

tion, the Peabody school-furniture business, its interests in the British Copperad heat convector company, an Italian WABCO foundry and its interest in the hydronic heating market and began extricating itself from several unprofitable heating enterprises in Europe.

When compared to the general recession gripping the world by 1975, American Standard "turned in an excellent performance," Marquard told stockholders. Income had again risen, reaching $44.8 million.[23] The company managed to top the previous year by reducing the taxes on its worldwide inventories. Managers switched to a "last-in, first-out [LIFO] inventory valuation," which eliminated the increased value of inventories driven by inflated material costs.[24]

Mosler's pneumatic tube, above, has become popular at bank drive-thru windows, below, which were also produced by the division.

Walking Away

Europe was a different story. There, American Standard labored under restrictive government controls and requirements as it tried to bring these subsidiaries in line. In France, conditions had deteriorated so far that Marquard's management team decided to simply leave. "Marquard has been ruthless," noted *Forbes* magazine in 1978, "and not only with Eberle's acquisitions."

"Take the building-products business in France, where American Standard had operated since around 1900. Its profitability dropped as French government controls on wages, prices and employment rose. American Standard abandoned all seven plants, more than $100 million in sales, and wrote off the $40 million assets."[25]

The heating business in Europe was still primarily cast-iron boilers and radiators, commented Roy Satchell, who was vice president of European plumbing and heating at the time. Not only did the plants in France need to be updated, but because of French laws, American Standard had been struggling from a weak position with union demands.

"I arrived at a time when we were sending a lot of new money in. We had several discussions with the French government because we wanted to shut down a couple of plants and move production into fewer plants to do it more economically, but we just didn't get anywhere. So we basically walked away from it, and the union workers 'occupied' the assets for several years."[26]

The French government handed the subsidiary over to a consortium of French manufacturers, and one of them eventually took control of the assets. "One of our French competitors took it over and shut down three plants. We only wanted to shut down two," Satchell said.

Marquard's management team decided to get out of the heating business in Europe, explained Cyril Gallimore, who was managing director of Ideal-Standard in Great Britain. He said his last job as director was to divest the English company, along with the marketing subsidiaries in

Belgium and Germany. "There was a lot of competition in that business, and working conditions in these foundries were not very pleasant, so American Standard decided to move out of it."[27]

Satchell recalled that feelings towards American executives became a little hairy, particularly in France and Italy, where union members occasionally kidnapped executives, only to release them a few hours later unharmed. "It was not uncommon in those days for that to happen," he said. "If the union didn't approve of what was going on, they would kidnap high-level executives and keep them prisoner for a while."[28] Satchell remembered when one executive in France was kidnapped, "workers shouted, 'To the melting pot with you!' The guy yelled back, 'Go ahead, you so-and-so's, you'll just spoil the metal!'" The executive was soon released.[29]

The consolidations had reduced the European workforce from about 15,000 employees to about 7,000, about half of those located in France.[30]

By 1977, the course set by Marquard seemed to be paying off. "Back in 1971, American Standard, Inc., so to speak, pulled the plug," stated a September 1977 *Barron's* article. "Accordingly, that year it set up a $120 million reserve — equal to $7.37 a share — to lop off low-margin or losing operations. The results since that fateful year ... have been impressive."[31]

Income had risen to $70.9 million in 1976 and saw a 24.6 percent increase the following year, to $88.4 million. American Standard was still the largest producer of plumbing products in the United States, but transportation and industrial products were just as important to the corporation. In 1976, for example, building products represented 35 percent of company sales while transportation and industrial products represented 34 percent.

Despite the nation's painful recession, American Standard was experiencing impressive growth. In 1978, revenues and income reached record levels. Sales exceeded $2 billion for the first time, and net income reached $101 million.

"Bill Marquard is running a pretty good show," *Forbes* magazine commented in 1978. "American Standard stock, which sold as low as $8 in 1975, now fetches $37 on the New York Stock Exchange. That's nearly double book value in a market that prices many companies like American Standard at substantial discounts."[32]

Part of the reason was that "construction and mining equipment, sold under the WABCO name, and the Mosler security and banking systems ... are both in improving markets," the magazine said.[33]

In 1979, American Standard was considered a major player in four industries: transportation products, building products, security and graphic products and construction and mining equipment. A more muscular American Standard operated in more than 20 countries and employed 51,000 people.

The Wall Street Journal forecast even better news for the company as orders for rail equipment began growing. From 1977 to 1978, orders for new railcars increased 95 percent, from 67,560 to 129,166.[34] Income in 1979 reached $132.2 million, with sales of $2.4 billion. American Standard was again breaking its own records. The company had reached its eighth year of uninterrupted earnings, and company officials stated that those kinds of numbers placed American Standard in the top 10 percent of U.S. industrial corporations "in terms of return on net worth."[35]

"We begin this new decade with confidence. Our company is stronger than at any time in its history," Marquard said at the close of the decade.[36] Once again economic conditions would challenge the company's re-emergence as a profitable enterprise. But in the dark days of the 1980s, American Standard would find a kindred spirit in The Trane Company, which was seeking shelter from a corporate raider.

By 1979, the transportation segment of the company had risen to more than $100 million.

The entire frame of this 170-ton construction and mining vehicle is being twisted to test its structural integrity.

CHAPTER TEN

A PERFECT FIT

1980–1987

"One out of every five bathrooms in the Free World is ours."

— William Marquard, 1980[1]

A *FORTUNE* MAGAZINE WRITER once noted that American Standard President and CEO William Marquard never let his face reveal his feelings. But the writer pointed out that Marquard had moved from wearing an austere expression in 1971, when he took over the troubled company, to a "four-color" smile by 1980.[2]

Marquard did have reason to smile as he sat in his office on the 21st floor of the company's New York City headquarters. That year, *Dun's Review* voted American Standard one of the five best-managed companies in the United States, along with Gannett, Intel, Perkin-Elmer and Standard Oil of Indiana.[3]

Marquard had successfully put the company on a corporate exercise plan and diet.[4] American Standard sold off $600 million in businesses, many of which had been returned to profitability and thus sold for book value or better, and streamlined the company into four major divisions: building products, transportation equipment, construction and mining equipment, and security and graphic products (essentially the Mosler Safe Division). "In effect, we deconglomerated," Marquard told *Forbes*, "and then reconsolidated into four worldwide businesses."[5]

By 1980, the Transportation Division was responsible for the bulk of American Standard's sales. Without squandering its energies on a mul-

titude of unrelated businesses, American Standard had achieved the objective started in the sixties under Eberle: the company's other industries helped insulate it from the vagaries of the construction market. The year 1980 broke records in terms of revenues and income, which reached $2.7 billion in sales and $157 million in earnings.[6]

The accomplishment was even more impressive considering the economic backdrop of high interest rates, which reached 20 percent, and runaway inflation that shrank the average paycheck. Internally, however, American Standard struggled with the opening of a new Steelcraft residential-steel-door plant and a fire that completely destroyed a plant in New Orleans. Newspaper accounts described the blaze as one of the "largest in the history of the city."[7] *The New York Times* carried a story and picture of the July 1980 blaze. One hundred fifteen firefighters, half of the New Orleans force, using two-thirds of the city's equipment, took part in battling the fire. In December 1980, the company made plans to rebuild the New Orleans pottery plant. At the time, the company had four other domestic pot-

As chairman and CEO, William Marquard turned American Standard around when it was strangling on its acquisitions.

tery plants in Torrance, California; Tiffin, Ohio; Trenton, New Jersey; and Plainfield, Connecticut.[8]

Trouble Coming

Marquard continued to emphasize cost-cutting because he foresaw that 1981 would bring even tougher conditions. In fact, the business environment was even worse than expected, as he candidly informed stockholders:

"I regret having to report American Standard's first earnings decline in 10 years. The Company's net income fell 19 percent in 1981 to $111 million. ... These results are a disappointment. ... Under the continued force of high inflation and high interest rates, these economies were much weaker than most had anticipated. Particularly hard hit were the automotive, railway and housing markets."[9]

Despite the setbacks of 1981, American Standard was number eight on *Financial World*'s list of the 25 fastest growth companies in the United States.[10] But the following year again lived down to Marquard's expectations. "The global business environment in 1982 was the worst since the Great Depression of the 1930s," he wrote gloomily to stockholders. "Our markets in all major industrialized countries declined, and some of the other countries — Canada, Mexico and Brazil, for example — suffered severe setbacks."[11]

American Standard was forced to freeze salaries and cut executive pay by 5 percent. By May 1982, the corporate staff was reduced 17 percent through early retirements and dismissals, and the workforce was reduced 15 percent, from 46,000 to 39,200.

American Standard was also hit with rising energy costs, but its conservation programs, which began in 1975 following the OPEC oil shock, softened the impact. In 1981, Martin Mozzo, director of energy management, said the company had set a goal of reducing its net energy consumption by 2 percent each year "by doing more than turning out lights." Mozzo said American Standard installed new meters, designed efficient distribution systems for utility services and provided adequate fuel storage. The company replaced energy-consuming equipment, such as older kilns in its pottery plants, with newer, more efficient models.[12]

1980 — American Standard once again breaks its own sales record by reaching $2.7 billion.

1982 — The company lays off staff and workers as conditions worsen.

1980

1981 — An unexpected recession results in the first earnings decline in 10 years.

1982 — IC Industries launches a hostile takeover bid for The Trane Company.

The Trane Acquisition

In his 1982 annual letter, Marquard told shareholders that American Standard still required basic restructuring to remain competitive. This meant reorganizing the company's businesses, further sell-offs in areas not related to its core strengths, and most significantly, re-entering the air conditioning market, where American Standard had suffered disappointment several times in its history. American Standard had first entered the market in the 1920s, but shut down its air conditioning business a decade later. The company tried the market again years later, but with only 5 percent of market share in 1975 American Standard abandoned the business. The capital required to keep growing the business was just too much.[13]

This time, American Standard looked to join forces with Wisconsin-based The Trane Company, a world leader in air conditioning, to combine its core competency with American Standard's long and successful history as a multinational corporation. For its part, The Trane Company found a white knight to save it from corporate raiders, most notably IC Industries, which had initiated a hostile takeover bid.[14]

IC Industries, a diversified railroad and consumer products conglomerate, had gradually purchased more than 24 percent of Trane's shares and announced plans to increase its holdings to just under 50 percent in 1983. Trane filed suit to block any further purchases and to force IC to divest its holdings in the company.[15] Trane also purchased General Electric's central air conditioning business in September 1982, a move that analysts speculated was made to dissuade IC from its course. The acquisition had a more important effect of opening up Trane's business to a much broader share, explained William Klug, a retired vice president and group executive for Trane. "It opened us up to the dealer-oriented, unitary market in the United States and gave us a whole different perspective on doing business in that area. That was a major change for the company."[16]

1984 — With markets improving, American Standard is able to rescue Trane.

1987 — American Standard, lean and strong, will soon face its greatest challenge in its history.

1987

1986 — Mosler is sold, along with other non-core businesses.

The construction industry's downturn did not diminish Trane's attractiveness. With more than $1 billion in annual sales, the company — with its workforce of 12,500 — was recognized as the prime innovator in its field. And Trane was both vulnerable and easy to disassemble: "We were cash-rich," explained George Kerckhove, who was division general manager at the time. "And our corporate structure would have made it easy for a raider to come in and spin off divisions because they stood alone. They were not integrated in any complex way."[17]

William Roth, then chairman and chief executive officer of Trane, wanted to merge with a company that shared Trane's values and management philosophy. American Standard looked to be a congenial fit. Both ran under a conservative corporate philosophy with a high emphasis on quality and durability. Both were open to new manufacturing processes and methods to boost efficiency, and both believed in dealing aboveboard, with honesty and integrity.

But until 1983, American Standard was unable to devote resources to a merger. When conditions somewhat improved that year, Marquard and Roth went ahead with the $500 million deal, which was completed in 1984. "It stretched us," recalled Marquard. "It really stretched us. As a matter of fact, there were some people in the company who were worried that we couldn't finance it. But it was the opportunity of a lifetime."[18]

Marquard had to approach IC Industries to purchase the 24 percent of shares it already owned. He and IC Chairman and CEO William Johnson sat down alone and hammered out a deal while attorneys from both companies waited in a hotel room down the street. "It was a long meeting," Marquard said. "I'll never forget it. We were in there until two o'clock in the morning."[19] American Standard paid part cash and part stock.

David Pannier, vice president and group executive of North American unitary air conditioning products, was relieved when American Standard finally put an end to the takeover attempt.

"I had a sense of relief that we were becoming part of a corporation that we felt would allow us to continue to grow our business and make the necessary investments to get that done, as opposed to slice us into little pieces and sell us off."[20]

A Crisp Partnership

As a corporate officer and division general manager at the time of the merger, Kerckhove believed it was important to maintain a separate brand image from American Standard to keep a high level of market share. "There was very little synergy on the manufacturing or sales side," he said. "The real synergy was the common philosophy of management and approach to the marketplace."[21]

Above left: William Roth, chairman and chief executive officer of Trane.

Above: The Trane Company installed this robot in its compressor assembly line in La Crosse, Wisconsin, to reduce costs and free humans from monotonous and repetitive tasks.

William Klug said American Standard was more oriented towards the balance sheet and managing cash flow, while Trane was more profit-and-loss oriented.[22] James Schultz, who was vice president of the refrigeration group at the time of the merger, agreed: "American Standard had pretty much left Trane alone from an operations standpoint, but it did bring a different financial outlook. It was much more into the financial analysis of projects than Trane was."[23]

The merger was complete on February 24, 1984, with Trane operating as a wholly owned subsidiary of American Standard. Trane's impact went further than just giving leadership in air conditioning to American Standard. Basically a domestic company that was international in scope, Trane reduced American Standard's risk in overseas markets, where fluctuating local currency against the dollar affected profits regardless of sales or price. In 1983, almost 40 percent of American Standard's sales came from the foreign markets; in one year that had fallen to less than 30 percent. "So long as the dollar remains strong we will benefit from having a higher proportion of our assets in areas not subject to the negative impact of currency translation," Marquard wrote to stockholders in 1984. "More important for the longer term is our enhanced position in the domestic U.S. market, which, we believe, will continue indefinitely to be the world's largest and the fastest growing."[24]

The merger was followed by more streamlining that continued under William Boyd, who became CEO when Marquard relinquished that post in 1985. Chief among the businesses to go was Mosler (part of the Security and Graphics Products Division) and American Bank Check (part of the American Bank Stationery Division). The decision to sell off these businesses was not an easy one, Boyd wrote in a letter to stockholders: "We deeply regret that some of these necessary actions will result in employment reductions. However, decisions of this kind must be made in

light of the long-term needs of all of our employees, stockholders and customers."[25]

Benson Stein, director of audits when Mosler and Bank Check were sold, said both companies "just didn't fit our strategy. I think we were into printing in a big way and it never really worked out that well for us. American Bank Check was one of many printing companies we disposed of."[26]

Interestingly enough, it was Kelso & Company that purchased Mosler. During the 1988 Black & Decker hostile takeover attempt, Kelso would serve as American Standard's white knight. Frank Nickell, president of Kelso, said he could understand why American Standard had decided to divest a profitable business such as Mosler.

"American Standard had decided to divest itself of companies that weren't core assets. Some of the stuff it had acquired over the years wasn't immediately relevant to its core businesses. Mosler fell into that category, and we bought the

Although profitable, the Mosler Safe Division did not fit into American Standard's core strengths, so it was sold to Kelso & Company in 1985.

Above: Years of trouble-free performance are made possible through American Standard's patented ceramic-disk closure technology and its washerless faucets.

Right: A 120-ton Haulpak truck hauling copper ore in Sonora, Mexico.

company at an auction staged by First Boston, whom American Standard had hired as agent."[27]

By the end of 1986, American Standard had sold off operating units with annual sales totaling about $600 million. The proceeds of the sales — 11 transactions in all — were used to pay off debt and repurchase 6.4 million shares of common stock. By the year's end, American Standard could be defined by three core businesses: air conditioning products, building products and transportation products.[28]

Marquard practiced his own form of divestiture when he stepped down as chairman in 1986,

with Boyd as his successor. Marquard continued as chairman of the company's executive committee and as a consultant. Boyd paid tribute to Marquard in March of that year:

"On January 1, 1986, William Marquard retired as chairman of the board after more than 30 years of service to the corporation and to the Mosler Safe Company before its acquisition by American Standard. Mr. Marquard became chief executive officer ... at a time of financial crisis. He put the company back on a firm financial footing."[29]

Changes at the Top

Boyd had been president and chief operating officer under Marquard for the previous two years. A graduate of Texas A&M University with a degree in mechanical engineering, Boyd served with General Electric Company for 20 years in a number of engineering, manufacturing and general management assignments. In 1967, he joined Carrier Corporation, Trane's biggest competitor, and rose to become president of Carrier

Air Conditioning Company as well as group vice president of the environmental systems group.

He moved over to American Standard in 1975 and served as group executive in charge of building products for the Western Hemisphere. Alan Root, who was director of business planning and marketing at the time, described Boyd's management style as "based on his experience, which was in manufacturing. He was a very down-to-earth individual and not given to fancy plans."[30]

Boyd continued the transactions started by Marquard to sell off Mosler and the security and graphics segments, and restructured the transportation segment in response to slow growth. In 1985, American Standard also opened a pottery plant in China, which it jointly owned with China's government. Total sales reached just under $3 billion with $196 million in income. New programs such as PRIDE (Personal Responsibility in Daily Efforts) and JIT (Just In Time manufacturing) reduced cost while increasing productivity and responsiveness to customer needs.

But American Standard's success brought unwanted attention in 1988. The dramatic battle that was shaping up with Black & Decker, determined to take over the company, underscored the dangers posed by the corporate-raider mentality of the eighties. American Standard would emerge battered and on the brink of bankruptcy.

Above left: Bill Boyd succeeded Marquard. His leadership skills would be tested by the Black & Decker takeover attack.

Above: WABCO's antilock braking system (ABS), which uses microprocessors to shorten stopping distances and improve steerability, had proven to be the most important innovation in commercial vehicle braking technology in the 1980s.

But certain initiatives started by Trane during this period would unlock American Standard's hidden strengths. Ultimately, these initiatives saved the corporation and put it on the path to success.

Trane confirmed actual performance of this 890-ton Model CVHE CenTraVac water chiller by means of a laboratory utilizing computer-controlled valves and the latest electronic instrumentation to simulate field conditions.

CHAPTER ELEVEN

TRANE

1885–1984

"While others in all lines of industry may have been contracting, Trane grasped the opportunity of building up its position."

— Reuben Trane, 1938[1]

TRANE AND AMERICAN Standard share many values because their founders were men of integrity. Such people tend to surround themselves with people possessing similar traits.

The Trane Company's origins begin with James Trane, a Norwegian immigrant who settled in La Crosse, Wisconsin, in 1864, where he worked as a steamfitter and plumber. In 1885, Trane opened his own plumbing shop and soon built a solid reputation as one of the area's most dependable and capable plumbers. As the business thrived, he moved to a downtown location in La Crosse in 1898, taking up three floors and the basement.[2]

Twelve years later, James' son, Reuben, joined him. Reuben had graduated with a degree in mechanical engineering, and he soon put his knowledge to use by tinkering with the existing heating system designs. With his father's help, Reuben designed a valve and trap system, to go into a new type of low-pressure steam heating invented by James.[3]

The innovative design showed immediate promise. In 1913, father and son incorporated as The Trane Company to manufacture this new line, which they called the Trane Vapor Heating System. They were joined by Emil Erickson, a master of manufacturing who helped cement a philosophy of manufacturing excellence, and Frank Hood. Hood would skillfully guide the company through times of boom and bust and would eventually succeed Reuben Trane as chairman of the corporation.

Three years following the debut of the Vapor Heating System, The Trane Company dropped out of the plumbing business completely, allowing the company's 10 workers to devote their full attention to building and improving upon their product.[4] Sales boomed as Trane Vapor Heating found application in both industrial and residential markets. By 1919, the company had a new plant built to turn out radiator traps, centrifugal pumps and other components that The Trane Company had previously purchased from other concerns. Reuben Trane had won a number of patents for innovative improvements on many of these components.

Relentlessly inventive, Reuben designed and built the convector radiator in 1925, an innovation that changed the face of the company. According to a report he wrote on May 21, he tested a copper sheet radiator comprising 12 pieces

James Trane, founder of The Trane Company.

of copper, and inserted 12 half-inch copper tubes, a much more efficient radiator design compared to the cast-iron radiator. "The advantages of this radiator would ... be that it would occupy about one-half the cubic contents per square foot of equivalent radiation, and the cost would be 37 percent of cast iron." The copper radiator weighed significantly less as well.[5]

Reuben Trane was concerned that the fledgling Trane Company was not equipped to manufacture the convector. In a curious twist of history, he offered it to industry giant American

1885 — James Trane opens a plumbing shop in La Crosse, Wisconsin. He moves downtown 13 years later.

1925 — Reuben Trane designs the convector radiator, which changes the industry.

1885

1913 — With his son, Reuben, James Trane incorporates as The Trane Company.

1931 — The company enters the air conditioning market with the Trane Unit Cooler.

Radiator Company. He was turned down. Undaunted, Reuben returned to Wisconsin, applied for a patent based on the radiator's new design and turned the energies of The Trane Company to producing it.

The design was described as "a copper heat tube bent into a U-shape upon which are mounted a multiplicity of spaced fins." Reuben also designed a special cabinet to help increase the flow of air through the radiator. Under the principle of convection, the radiator heats air as it passes over the heating element (which was made of copper tubes and fins in Reuben's design), and the heated air then rises to the outlet grill at the top of the cabinet to warm the room.

The company touted the convector as "the lightweight successor to the cast-iron radiator," and it quickly caught on with many segments of the building industry, including architects con-

Opposite page: Trane opened his own plumbing shop at 118 Pearl Street in downtown La Crosse, Wisconsin, in 1885.

Right: The convector radiator was a hit across the construction industry.

cerned with aesthetics; engineers concerned with practicality; and contractors, the people who actually had to install the units. Sales offices that had already spread across the country multiplied further, and a Canadian subsidiary was established in 1928 in Toronto, spreading Trane products throughout the British Empire. By 1930,

1939 — The Turbovac is introduced.

1983 — Trane becomes the target of a hostile takeover.

1984

1954 — Reuben Trane dies.

1984 — Trane officially becomes part of American Standard.

Trane's first engineering graduates, the class of 1925.

sales at the parent company had topped $2 million for the first time.[6]

Another innovation by Reuben Trane helped assure the convector radiator's success — he launched what today is called the Trane Graduate Engineer Training Program in 1926. The first of its kind (and widely acknowledged today as the industry's finest), the program recruited engineering graduates from respected colleges and universities to enter an intensive postgraduate training regimen that included sales and engineering. (Later, the program would expand to include HVAC systems design and application.) Successful graduates of the six-month program advanced to sales or management assignments.[7]

Trane first entered the air conditioning market when it introduced the Trane Unit Cooler in 1931. Like the convector radiator, the unit cooler blew air past coils cooled by circulating water and found application in offices, restaurants, shops, department stores and factories. But the Great Depression paralyzed the construction industry. Sales for all products, heating and cooling, fell off

sharply. Like many American businesses, Trane required a combination of ingenuity and employee loyalty to survive the economic malaise.[8]

In three years, sales went from the high of $2.1 million to just $841,000. Workers such as Roland Stange, a production supervisor and one who was single at the time, took time off so men with families could keep working. When conditions improved, Stange rejoined the workforce. Conditions slowly improved, and by 1936 new construction helped Trane recover lost ground.

The Turbovac

Conditions turned for the worse again in 1938, with the air conditioning market coming to a virtual standstill. The term "recession" was coined to distinguish the latest downturn from the Depression. After six years of pumping federal money into the moribund economy, President Roosevelt, worried over rising deficits and inflation, ordered deep spending cuts. The economy was struck again when the Treasury Department began to collect Social Security taxes directly from employee paychecks, which immediately reduced disposable income. (Social Security was in its infancy, having been enacted in 1935.)

Sales across the industry declined by a whopping 44 percent. Heating suffered to a lesser extent, and since most of Trane's sales came from the heating side of the market, sales fell just 20 percent. Income, however, was cut in half, from $397,000 to $196,600. That the company showed any profit was a testament to its conservative fiscal policies, a practice that is a hallmark of Trane today.

Reuben Trane emphatically explained — in capital letters in the 1938 Annual Report — why stockholders should consider the year "no ordinary milestone in the history of the company."

"The officers and directors, though somewhat disappointed, WANT YOU TO KNOW THAT THE COMPANY IS ONE OF THE RELATIVELY FEW IN THE AIR CONDITIONING INDUSTRY TO REPORT ANY PROFIT WHATSOEVER. AS A MATTER OF FACT, SO FAR AS IS KNOWN BY US, THE DOLLAR PROFIT RECORDED BY THE COMPANY IS THE LARGEST RECORDED BY ANY COMPANY IN THE FIELD REGARDLESS OF THE SIZE PRODUCING A SIMILAR LINE OF PRODUCTS."[9]

Trane's executives knew that opportunity was building in the construction industry. Reuben Trane told stockholders that "while others in all lines of industry may have been contracting, Trane grasped the opportunity of building up its position."[10] The downturn, like all downturns, would eventually end and the volatile air conditioning market would rebound with a need for a modern way to cool water for air conditioning systems. Chilled water had previously come from wells or intricately unreliable water-over-ice sprays and cooling towers. The introduction of a chemical refrigerant, known by the DuPont tradename Freon-12, revolutionized the air conditioning industry in 1930. Developed through the cooperative research effort of Frigidair, General Motors and DuPont, Freon-12

The CenTraVac water chiller evolved from the highly successful Turbovac, introduced in 1939. The CenTraVac (pictured here under construction in 1955) became the industry standard for large commercial air conditioning units.

met the goal of being safe for use in homes: It was odorless, nonflammable, nontoxic and did not corrode. But water chiller equipment was complicated, expensive to maintain and often unreliable.

Addressing these nagging problems, Trane in early 1939 introduced the Turbovac, the industry's first hermetically sealed centrifugal water chiller. Designed for large commercial applications, the Turbovac represented a large portion of Trane's research and development effort. The company worked closely with consulting engineers and mechanical contractors to develop a system that was efficient and easy to maintain and could be installed with a minimum of help from the manufacturer.[11]

Above: Although the U.S. mainland was never in danger of air attack, blackout ventilators hid the lights of coastal factories from enemy submarines.

Right: Wood frames were used for Trane products when metal became scarce.

Below: The aircraft intercooler was used in fighters and bombers, and allowed aircraft to reach higher altitudes. Pictured here is a P-47 Thunderbolt fighter. Background: The intercooler was used in the B-24 Liberator bomber as well.

The Turbovac was introduced carefully and on a limited basis, but the results were so gratifying that Trane began tooling up for anticipated orders in 1939, the year the company recorded $5 million in sales for the first time. The Turbovac program gradually expanded and became the forerunner of the CenTraVac centrifugal water chiller, introduced in 1951. Between 1939 and 1997, more than 30,000 Turbovac and CenTraVac units would be sold, capturing 50 percent of the market.

The Turbovac and many other Trane products found ready acceptance on military bases and in factories working around the clock following the December 7, 1941, Japanese attack on Pearl Harbor. An ingenious combination of coils and the Turbovac, for example, proved a highly effective method to improve steel mill efficiency by removing moisture from the air in blast furnaces. By doing so, the output, quality and uniformity of steel were increased without having to build new blast furnaces from scratch.[12] In addition, Trane engineers designed and installed blackout ventilators, which kept air circulating in facto-

ries around the clock while hiding lights.[13] Though the United States mainland was never in danger of air raid, the device was useful in factories located on both coasts because enemy submarines often used city lights as navigational guides.

But the aircraft intercooler was Trane's most significant contribution to the war effort. The aircraft intercooler allowed U.S. aircraft to fly at higher altitudes and avoid antiaircraft fire. Fighter pilots also had the advantage of diving to attack the enemy unexpectedly from above. The project was shrouded in wartime secrecy at a footwear factory leased for this purpose in La Crosse. By 1942, The Trane Company's production went totally toward filling wartime needs.

Peacetime Expansion

Peace brought unparalleled prosperity to the nation. The Trane Company was in an enviable position to take advantage of the construction boom stimulated by millions of returning veterans and their families, the precursor to the baby boom. Double-digit increases in volume became common every year throughout the postwar period. Factories were added, and sales offices opened all over the world, directed by Donald C. Minard, Reuben Trane's successor in 1951. Reuben Trane had been president of The Trane Company for 38 years. He stepped aside to became chairman of the company's first board of directors.

Minard had risen through the ranks. A member of the first graduating engineer class, he took on more and more responsibilities through the years. Following World War II, he established sales offices strategically in and outside the United States by helping independent franchise holders to open offices and then encouraging them to establish service organizations. The service organizations took care of equipment startup and warranty claims and eventually moved into sales of parts. The engineers at these service centers underwent extensive training by the company.[14]

Reuben Trane retired as chairman in 1953 and was succeeded by Frank Hood. Reuben died a year later, on September 5, but his legacy continued to prosper. By 1958, the year Trane's stock began trading on the New York Stock Exchange, net sales had risen to $81.5 million,

Reuben Trane died September 5, 1954, but he left a legacy of engineering excellence and success.

with $6 million in earnings, and Trane entered the residential air conditioning market.

Two years later, sales reached a record $102 million as Trane solidified its position in the HVAC industry. Air conditioning products, the fastest growing market, were installed in military and civilian projects that ranged from skyscrapers to underground missile silos. (Trane won a commendation from the Army Corps of Engineers for its role in the Titan project in 1962.) Compact air conditioners were used on mobile military equipment as well. Seattle's famous "Space Needle," built for the 1962 World's Fair and cooled by Trane products, was another high-profile application.[15] Absorption water chillers, centrifugal refrigeration units and reciprocating units were installed throughout the world, from Beirut to Germany. Trane opened offices on the

Apollo 15 was the first moon mission to utilize the Lunar Rover. The rover was equipped with Trane-designed heat exchangers.
(Photo courtesy of NASA.)

Continent to take advantage of the European Common Market, the economic association that sprang up in the wake of World War II. The Common Market helped liberalize trade policies that led to economic prosperity in Western Europe, which meant people had the resources to improve their lives with air conditioning. By the end of 1971, sales from the International Division had mushroomed beyond $50 million (almost 20 percent of the Trane's total sales of $259 million), and sales offices and distributors in 91 nations.

Reaching for the Moon

Trane engineering broke the bonds of Earth when Apollo 15 touched down on the moon in 1971. The Lunar Rover that sped across the surface of the moon was equipped with a Trane-designed specialized brazed aluminum heat exchanger, similar to the design used during World War II in the aircraft intercooler. George Kerckhove, who helped develop the heat exchanger, recalled that 21 units were built to function with a special paraffin-type wax designed to melt in the sun and solidify in the dimmer moonlight, creating a stabilizing effect for the transmission of the television picture seen from the moon.[16]

The Apollo 15 project and other innovations led to the formation of the Process Division. The division had the responsibility for making use of the new technologies for commercial applications. The division landed a major contract with the U.S. Atomic Energy Commission for the brazed aluminum heat exchangers to improve the government's method of purifying uranium to be used as nuclear fuel. Trane's project team developed a unique curved design for the exchanger. The configuration exceeded the commission's expectations, and within several years, the Process Division was designing and building other components for use in nuclear reactors.[17]

But the promise of nuclear power in the seventies did not satisfy the world's growing appetite for fossil fuels. (Nuclear power would eventually fall into disfavor as concern grew over its safety. Plummeting oil prices in the eighties made nuclear power seemingly unnecessary, and it became undesirable to people, so the Process Division exited the market.) The OPEC oil embargo of 1973 shocked Americans into the realization that they depended on foreign countries, many of them unstable, for their energy needs. Energy conservation had been growing as a public policy debate and now took on immediate importance.

Trane engineers had been looking for ways to cut down energy consumption three years prior to the embargo. Writing to shareholders, Trane Chairman and CEO Thomas Hancock noted that Trane had put greater emphasis on reducing energy consumption in existing products as well as in new lines. Trane introduced the energy-saving computerized program called Trane Air Conditioning Economics (or TRACE), which allows customers to decide on the most economic fuel, equipment and building designs to heat and cool a building. A two-stage residential air conditioner reduced energy usage by 30 to 40 percent. New features such as a variable air volume product made existing systems more efficient.[18]

Hancock confidently told stockholders in the mid-seventies that the air conditioning industry "is in the midst of a new, exciting and highly productive era of perhaps as broad significance and as great importance as any since it came into its own some 20 years ago."

"It is a ... wave engulfing all elements of the industry — the architectural and engineering professions, contractors and manufacturers. It is producing significant increases in the value of air conditioning to the owner by reducing the amount of cooling required to air condition most buildings, making more efficient use of energy and generally improving importance and reliability."[19]

The Central Air Conditioning Acquisition

The search for more efficient air conditioning designs continued in the early 1980s. The three-stage CenTraVac chiller was a major innovation, one that solidified Trane's position as the leader in centrifugal chillers. But for years Trane executives wanted to find a way to gain a strong presence in the central residential air conditioning business. In 1982, a rare opportunity to do so presented itself when General Electric decided to sell off its Central Air Conditioning Division to free up cash for other high-technology endeavors.

Trane purchased the division for $135 million in cash. Analysts speculated that Trane purchased the division in part to ward off a number of unfriendly takeover attempts, but they failed to recognize (or at least acknowledge) the unique advantages offered by the former G.E. unit. Chairman and CEO William Roth spelled out these advantages in a *New York Times* article shortly after the purchase, and time has since borne him out: "[Trane received a] successful line of complements to existing lines, the volume necessary to bring costs on small air-conditioners into line with those of competitors, a 5,500-dealer network of retail outlets that would have cost $50 million to build, readily transferable technology and three up-to-date manufacturing facilities (in Tyler, Texas; Trenton, New Jersey; and Fort Smith, Arkansas)."[20] The acquisition boosted Trane annual sales by an additional $260 million. Trane CAC, Inc., became the leading manufacturer of heat pumps and ranked number two overall in its markets in the United States.

If the acquisition was indeed made to thwart takeover attempts, as was asserted, it failed. In 1983, Trane passed the $1 billion mark in sales. That year, IC Industries launched a sustained attack on Trane. This time, Roth decided to find a white knight. He and William Marquard of American Standard had discussed merging in the past, but it wasn't until 1983, when sales and net income improved, that American Standard had the resources to complete the acquisition. Trane officially became part of American Standard on February 24, 1984.

From that time to 1998, Trane has grown from $1.2 billion in sales to $3.6 billion, with an incredible increase in net income from $65 million to $364 million, making it the most profitable segment of American Standard.

Made of re-engineered acrylic, this is no ordinary bathtub. By 1993, the year this image ran in a remodeling catalog, American Standard had re-engineered itself as well. Both became tougher.

CHAPTER TWELVE

FIGHTING BACK– THE DFT REVOLUTION

1988–1998

"If Demand Flow Technology works, it will save us. If it doesn't, we will go bankrupt."

— Emmanuel Kampouris, 1990[1]

O N JANUARY 26, 1988, THE FOLLOW-ing letter from Black & Decker's chairman and CEO, Nolan D. Archibald, arrived on the desk of William Boyd, chairman and CEO of American Standard. The letter was simul-taneously distributed to business editors around the nation:

"Dear Mr. Boyd: Over the past several months I have tried to arrange a meeting with you to discuss a business combination between the Black & Decker Corporation and American Standard, Inc. ... I was hopeful that you would meet me to discuss this combination and was disappointed that you were not willing even to listen to a plan that will serve the best interests of our companies and their constituencies. As we remain convinced that the merits of the plan deserve consideration, our only alternative is to take our proposal directly to American Standard's stockholders. Accordingly, the board of directors of Black & Decker has approved an all-cash tender offer, which will commence today, for all outstanding shares of American Standard at $56 per share. ..."[2]

The takeover bid, eerily reminiscent of IC's takeover attempt of Trane, surprised business analysts and investors. "There are no obvious synergies," noted one analyst. "Black & Decker is a consumer company turning into a conglomerate. This muddies the waters."[3]

Archibald made his first over-ture through an investment banker from Shearson Lehman Hutton, who contacted a member of American Standard's board in the fall of 1987. Archibald then called Boyd person-ally. "We've been rebuffed three times," Archibald told *Business Week*. "I called Bill Boyd and told him his shareholders could receive a substantial premium with the combination of our two companies."[4]

But the cost would be high to American Standard. Archibald let it be known that Black & Decker intended to dismember WABCO by selling it off for $600 million, allow Trane to operate on its own, and weave in the plumbing fixture lines to complement its own building products line.

"The feeling all along in the plumbing side was that Black & Decker had one thing in mind, and that was to fully integrate our faucet and fixture business," said Adrian Deshotel, vice president of human resources, in a 1998 interview.

This thinker is deep in thought on a Heritage-style toilet in a Shanghai showroom.

"This would have a major impact on the business as we knew it. We in plumbing would be thrown into upheaval, and there would be job losses and things like that. There was a lot of tension in the plumbing business at the time."[5]

To avoid being acquired by the Towson, Maryland, manufacturer of small appliances and power tools, American Standard would again take on heavy debt and seek its own white knight, with repercussions lasting well into the next decade.

"American Standard was a successful company and had a lot of cash," said Benson Stein, who was audit director at the time. "Even people within the corporation felt that we had to do something to make an acquisition or return funds to shareholders. Out of the blue, Black & Decker made a bid for American Standard."[6]

Black & Decker had emerged from its own troubles to become an aggressive force. Under Archibald, it restructured the Power Tools Division and successfully engineered a change in brand names (considered one of the most difficult marketing feats) without losing market share when it purchased the Small Appliance Division from General Electric.[7] One article noted that Black & Decker had become "cocky" in its ability to hold onto market share and at the same time improve profitability of a new division. "We think we've made a real name for ourselves over the last year or two as an innovative marketer and new-product company," one Black & Decker spokesman was quoted as saying. "We thought we could bring the same energy and growth to American Standard."[8]

In covering Black & Decker's relentless takeover attempt, *Business Week* noted that it was "small wonder, perhaps, that one of B&D's best-selling products is the line of Piranha circular saw blades."[9]

Reactions

Robert Wellbrock was walking to the train with his newspaper on January 27, 1988, the day after Nolan Archibald released his letter to the press. Wellbrock, an executive in the tax department, had been working at American Standard for just three months when he opened the newspaper and discovered his new employer was under attack.

"I follow Black & Decker because the head of their tax department had worked with me at

1988 — Black & Decker causes American Standard's stock to rise to $65 a share.

1988 — Black & Decker hesitates, then decides to give up. American Standard ceases to operate as a public company.

1988

1988 — After maneuvering by both companies, American Standard stock hits $72.75 a share. Kelso & Company eventually offers $78 a share.

another large company. My reaction was, 'Holy mackerel, we're a target!' One of the reasons I came to American Standard was because it was a large, conservative, well-capitalized company, and I had already gone through this experience at other companies. I thought, 'Here I go again.'"[10]

Black & Decker had launched its no-holds-barred attempt to acquire American Standard through the newspapers. Black & Decker offered the company $56 per share or $1.8 billion — an offer considered much too low by analysts at the time.

William Boyd recommended that the stockholders reject the bid. "Here we have American Standard with $3.4 billion of sales in 1987 and return on equity for stockholders at 16.2 percent after tax. That puts us in the top quartile of companies," he said, pointing out that Black & Decker was in the lower quartile with return on equity of about 8.8 percent.[11]

Black & Decker upped the ante a few weeks later when it offered $65 a share, or $2.1 billion. Boyd again turned the offer down and urged stockholders to do the same in a letter dated February 9, 1988. The board of directors, mean-

while, passed a "poison pill" defense, which essentially gave stockholders a limited opportunity to buy American Standard stock at $32.50 a share (half the price of Black & Decker's offer). The special price would be triggered if a bidder acquired 15 percent or more of stock. Such a move was designed to make the company's remaining shares of stock prohibitively expensive.[12]

Anticipating higher bids from Black & Decker, American Standard secured $1.9 billion from four banks (Chemical Bank, Citibank, the Manufacturers Hanover Trust Company and the Sumitomo Bank, Ltd., of Japan) in late February 1988 and launched a recapitalization plan to refinance the company and pay out a sizable dividend to shareholders.

One of American Standard's suppliers, Emerson Electric Company, kicked in $160 million in March to help the recapitalization plan in exchange for a 10 percent stake in the company and an agreement to sell unspecified products to American Standard. The plan pushed American Standard stock to more than $72 a share, largely in securities. That a supplier would help shore up American Standard came as a surprise to many investors, particularly because Emerson dis-

1995 — Turning itself around, American Standard becomes a public company again.

1998

1990 — With a recession threatening, debt-laden American Standard launches a new manufacturing initiative called Demand Flow Technology.

1997 — American Standard achieves $6 billion in sales.

Faucets and other accessories from American Standard's Sottini Azimuth Collection, above, shine with the originality of European designers, while the Ideal Standard shower fixtures, below, show off simplicity of design.

avowed any notion that it intended to try to acquire American Standard.

Relentless Pursuit

Within hours of the announcement, Black & Decker came back with a bigger surprise: Archibald offered $72.75 a share, or $2.3 billion — and all in cash, as opposed to American Standard's offer. "Black & Decker appeared to have assessed the market value of American Standard's complex proposal and then bid slightly higher," noted *The New York Times*. "Wall Street professionals are widely known to prefer cash to any other payment."[13]

On the front line, the investment houses advising the gladiators were watched as well: "The battle is also a test of the takeover skills of two of Wall Street's leading investment houses, the old-line Goldman, Sachs & Company [advising American Standard] and the increasingly entrepreneurial Shearson Lehman Hutton [advising Black & Decker]."

The hallways of American Standard's headquarters buzzed with rumors and worry as information broke and then became obsolete, recalled Angela Tripodi, an assistant to Vice President and

General Counsel Richard Kalaher. "I was in the legal department, and things were going hot and heavy. Faxes were coming in every day with what was happening. Everybody was upset because we really didn't know what was going to happen to us."[14]

In March, Archibald accused American Standard of unfair play because the target erected barriers to preserve its independence. Archibald also publicly dispelled rumors of a cease-fire that were circulating throughout the financial community, although he said Black & Decker had offered to "forgo a street sweep for a time period if American Standard would agree ... to withdraw its poison pill."

"We continue to believe American Standard's directors should provide a level playing field. If they wish to provide a level playing field, they must remove the poison pill so that our offer can compete with their recapitalization plan. Also, they must make the $80 million in excess pension plan assets available to all bidders, not just to their plan. Finally, they must eliminate the excessive golden parachute and other benefits that would be triggered by an acquisition by Black & Decker, but not by their plan. ... The directors of American Standard have a duty to offer the company's stockholders a chance to accept it by dismantling the barriers they have raised. If they do not, we will continue to solicit consents of their stockholders to remove them."[15]

The "excessive golden parachute and other benefits" referred to a proposed employee stock ownership plan (ESOP) that would have boosted the management and employee benefit plan stake from 4 percent to 52 percent

if an outsider attempted to acquire the company. Black & Decker filed an injunction with the federal district court in Wilmington, Delaware, insisting that the plan undermined its bid for American Standard. The court agreed, stating that the ESOP plan constituted a sale of American Standard. That being the case, "American Standard's board must not give preferential treatment to one bidder over another," wrote Judge Joseph Longobardi in a 39-page opinion.[16]

Black & Decker had the green light to press its attack home, but another player had entered the arena.

Enter Kelso & Company

The New York Times once wrote that Louis Kelso, founder and chairman of the investment banking firm Kelso & Company, "wastes no love on Wall Street. 'We have to take capital ownership out of that gambling casino,' he says."[17]

Kelso & Company joined the fray prior to the court's injunction against American Standard. When Judge Longobardi ruled that the recapitalization plan was actually a sale, Kelso stepped in as a serious bidder, recalled Kelso President Frank Nickell. Kelso had purchased two business units from American Standard (one of them being Mosler), and its management knew William Marquard well.

"We and Bill Marquard had developed a good relationship, and we had a fond place in our heart for American Standard because of the two companies we bought from them. We always had a lot of respect for American Standard because they had always been reasonable and honest."[18]

Since the court ruled that American Standard was essentially up for sale to the highest bidder, Black & Decker had to contend with Kelso & Company if it wanted to prevail. For Kelso & Company, the multibillion-dollar battle was by far the biggest it had undertaken to save a company from predators. Its largest deal to date was Blue Bell, Inc., a maker of Wrangler jeans and other apparel, for $660 million. Blue Bell was later sold — intact — to VF Corporation for $775 million. "Unlike many firms that specialize in leveraged

buyouts," noted *The New York Times*, "Kelso has a record of keeping the companies it buys intact."[19]

The late Louis Kelso, an economist and lawyer, founded the investment firm in 1968. He pioneered the concept of ESOP in the 1950s when he helped the employees of a California newspaper find a way to buy the business when the owner decided to retire. The owner gave his employees the first crack at buying the newspaper before offering it for sale, but the employees could not finance the loans without risking their savings and their homes. Kelso engineered an ESOP plan that allowed the employees to buy 72 percent of the newspaper's stock. The ESOP plan was first disguised as an employee benefits plan, thus avoiding "confronting a deeply entrenched national economic policy committed to toil and welfare for the many and capital ownership for the few," as described in Kelso's book, *Democracy and Economic Power: Extending the ESOP Revolution.*[20]

Kelso, 74 years old at the time of the Black & Decker fight, devoted much of his time to lecturing and writing about the need for workers to share in stock ownership of corporations as a way to put the American Dream within the average worker's reach. He believed that by giving the average worker a sizable stake in a democratized capitalistic economy, the goals of widespread personal prosperity, technological progress, corporate efficiency and national growth would be achieved.

Kelso & Company had approached Goldman, Sachs & Company in February while the latter investment house was putting together American Standard's recapitalization plan. As the bidding escalated, American Standard disclosed that it was negotiating a friendly buyout with an unnamed suitor. Soon it was known that Kelso was offering $76 a share for American Standard, a $2.5 billion deal.

Once again, Black & Decker fired back with a tender offer of $77, but Kelso was prepared to fight it out and declared it was ready to up its own offer.

"We didn't come this far to be deterred by this kind of response," asserted Joseph Schuchert, Kelso's managing partner. "We'll tender at $78 and see what they do. If it's necessary to bump up our tender offer, that's what we'll do."[21] Kelso had its own fund but took the precaution of lining up several more participants, including First Boston Corporation, which provided $900 million in temporary financing. "It went right down to the wire," recalled former General Counsel John Geer. "The bids were within $1 of each other when, in the middle of the night, Black & Decker gave up."[22]

On March 22, 1988, Black & Decker withdrew its offer to purchase American Standard for $77 a share after Kelso agreed to pay Black & Decker $25 million to drop its bid. The payment covered expenses incurred by Black & Decker in its takeover attempt. Archibald explained that his company "made a commitment to our stockholders that when the bidding reached the level where it was not consistent with Black & Decker's aggressive earnings per share and return-on-equity growth objectives, we would not pursue it."[23]

ASI, a holding company formed by Kelso, bought 29.6 million, or 95 percent, of American Standard's outstanding shares for $3 billion in April 1988. On July 5, 1988, the merger was completed when Kelso acquired the remaining 31.5 million shares at $78 a share. American Standard became a privately owned company.

"It was a monumental experience for the company," said Henry Steiner, former general counsel. "It required a view that was totally different from anything that had gone before. The strain and the effort necessary to raise the money to do a leveraged buyout on a bootstrap basis imposed on us a totally new and very challenging atmosphere."[24]

It was one that came with a hefty price tag. After the buyout, American Standard's debt service alone was $300 million per year, or nearly $1 million per day. Analysts at the time stated that the buyout would leave American Standard once again facing huge debts. One analyst said American Standard would have a negative book value.

There were personal sacrifices for employees, too. The pension plan for salaried employees was replaced with an ESOP that gave workers a 20 percent stake in the company, said Raymond Pipes, vice president of investor relations. "There was a lot of nervousness about the future at that point," he said.

"We had to manage things in a very different way. Automatically providing for future pensions is quite a significant cost. Replacing that with something that is driven off the value of the company stock, and is linked to the performance of the company, was not a bad idea, but it added to the state of nervousness and apprehension. It clearly marked a change in the company."[25]

An even bigger change would be needed if American Standard was to survive.

Bill Boyd decided to step down from all posts in January 1989 as his age of retirement approached. Kelso & Company executives thanked him for the job he did in fighting off the hostile takeover.

American Standard, struggling to pay its debt while carrying on diverse manufacturing operations, had millions of dollars tied up in stock and parts inventory.

DEMAND FLOW TECHNOLOGY

Demand Flow Technology has revolutionized manufacturing by dramatically reducing the practice of staging production in different parts of a factory. At the top, color-coded Operation Method Sheets make sure each product has been inspected several times at various checkpoints as the product is assembled. During the subassembly process, shown in the middle picture, the pace of operation is set to maintain a one-piece flow with the assembly line. The production team, right, tears off color-coded cards from a board each time a part is used in the sub-assembly process. Orange indicates the need to order new parts from the supplier.

American Standard was in need of a leader, so William Marquard returned as chairman. Marquard quickly recommended that Emmanuel A. Kampouris join him as president and chief executive officer. "When Kelso came and asked me, I backed Kampouris as the fellow that ought to go in," Marquard said.[26]

Called "Mano" by almost everyone who knows him, Oxford-educated, Egyptian-born Kampouris joined a Greek subsidiary of American Standard in 1966 as general manager and rose to become its managing director in 1970. He became senior vice president of the Building Products sector in 1989. Colin Wise, retired financial head of the European plumbing unit, said Kampouris demonstrated a very astute and educated vision, which he was capable of communicating in several languages — Italian, Greek, Arabic, French and English. His promotion to CEO (and chairman in 1993) was the "biggest and best final change" to occur at American Standard prior to Fred Jaqua's retirement in 1996 as vice president and special counsel.

Kampouris turned to DFT to find a way to use the company's working capital (money tied up in inventory) to pay down its debt without drastically curtailing operations.

"He brought in a marvelous respect for the people who actually do things, who make the products, and the people who go out and sell them. And he has a totally open, flexible mind, always interested in refining and perfecting the things that were working and the things that weren't working."[28]

Kampouris asked a critical question as he assumed the company's reins — what would happen to American Standard if the nation plunged into a recession? An analysis provided the answer in stark and brutal terms. "We wouldn't be able to keep the company together," he explained. With more than $3.1 billion in junk bonds compared with $3.4 billion in sales, "we were maxed out from a debt standpoint. We would have to starve the company to service the debt."[29]

The sudden spike in fuel prices resulting from Iraq's invasion of Kuwait in 1990 pushed the American economy into a tailspin. The theoretical model became a chilling reality. Kampouris realized that much of the company's cash was tied up as working capital. The company maintained huge inventories of parts that often corroded before they could be used to finish a product, noted *Fortune* in 1994. The magazine used Trane as an example of the problem common throughout the company.

Demand Flow at American Standard 1991–1995

	1991	1992	1993	1994	1995
Inventory Turnover*:	4.9x	6.0x	7.5x	9.7x	10.7x
Operating Working Capital as a Percent of Sales:**	8.6	7.5	5.9	4.9	4.9
Net Cash Provided by Operating Activities ($millions):	241	174	201	257	348

*Following year's first quarter projected cost of sales annualized, divided by adjusted inventories as of December 31.

**Operating working capital as of December 31, divided by annualized fourth-quarter sales. Operating working capital is defined as net accounts receivable and adjusted inventories less accounts payable, accrued payrolls, and other accrued liabilities.

Source: Company reports.

CHART ADAPTED FROM *Chief Executive* MAGAZINE.

American Standard's achievement in reaching zero working capital landed it and Kampouris on the cover of many business magazines, including *Chief Executive*.

"These parts spent only a few hours — or minutes — on the machines but sat in mountainous inventories for weeks; certain specialized parts remained for months or years. ... When an order came in, Trane needed an average of 15 days to find the components and assemble the final unit. Incredibly, despite the vast inventories, Trane often didn't have or couldn't find the parts it needed. Those pulled from stocks often turned out to be damaged. Many items rusted on the blacktop or took a bang from the forklift."[30]

American Standard had few options to service its debt. It could sell off huge chunks of the company (which most likely would have happened if the company lost the takeover battle) or it could somehow use the money tied up in inventory. The latter solution was obviously the best, and Kampouris asked one of his executives, Gary Biddle, to find a way to move product through manufacturing to the customer more quickly without sacrificing quality.

At the same time, executives from Trane's Unitary Product Group had begun to implement a new process called Demand Flow Technology after attending classes taught by John Costanza, founder, president and CEO of JCIT and author of *The Quantum Leap in Speed to Market*. Demand Flow was an outgrowth of Just In Time manufacturing. "Cash flow was king," noted David Pannier, vice president and group executive of Air Conditioning Unitary Products. "It was a matter of survival. We had to turn inventory into cash."[31]

Trane's plant in Tyler, Texas, was one of the first areas where DFT had gone into effect. Pannier commented that Demand Flow Technology required a mental and physical restructuring to get the right pieces of equipment in place.

"It is not the repetitive motion-type of assembly process you might have expected or that we in fact used. Line workers had to learn how to do the job of the person in front of them and do the job of the person downstream of them. So if we saw that a bottleneck was forming in the assembly line, people could shift to those areas of the assembly line where they were needed, and they had to have the skills to go and help someone get past the bottleneck."[23]

Lead times at all stages began to shrink. Orders no longer took as long as 10 days to wander through six departments before actually getting to the shop floor, where another laborious process (15 days on average) would ensue.

In 1990, Kampouris noticed the effect DFT was having on Trane's Tyler facility. By then, conditions had gotten to the point where executives began looking into selling off WABCO, which was exactly what would have happened under Black & Decker. "Mano saw a way to use DFT as a vehicle to take working capital out of the company and use it to service the debt, while keeping American Standard intact," remarked John Costanza in a 1998 interview. "It takes a real gutsy CEO to see it and then do it."

"A lot of people internally, even at the executive level, said it couldn't be done and that they ought to start selling off pieces of the company. Mano said they were not going to break the company up. 'We're going to build a more responsive company and have a greater value for all.'"[32]

Kampouris acknowledged that his decision to convert the company to DFT was based on "the wrong reason."[33] His original goal was to move inventory out fast to bring in enough cash to run the business. DFT, improved upon with software developed specifically for the company, is now applied with the singular goal of keeping American Standard flexible so it can deliver to the customer what he wants and when he wants it.

Such a radical change had to be zealously supported by the corporation's leadership. Cyril Gallimore, who retired as vice president of systems and technology in 1997, said "it was made very clear to managers right from the top that if they weren't willing to get on the bandwagon, they should look elsewhere for a job because this was what we were going to do."[34]

Kampouris was more to the point: "If Demand Flow Technology works," he told his top executives in February 1990, "it will save us. If it doesn't, we will go bankrupt."[35]

Turning Around

American Standard committed $100 million to convert its 85 facilities in 32 countries to DFT, using the Tyler plant as a model for the rest of the company. Others soon followed, including the plant in La Crosse, Wisconsin. James Schultz, vice president and business leader of Worldwide Applied Systems, sat in John Costanza's class with his management team from La Crosse. He recalled that their first reaction was the typical one when confronted with the need to change methods: "We looked at it, and we talked about it. Then we argued about it and we denied it."[35]

"There's a denial period. 'This won't work in our business. We're unique.' You have to break that down because it will work in your business and you aren't unique. So we came back after a week and picked a spot and started working on it."[36]

The compressor side of the manufacturing department at La Crosse was selected as one of the places to begin. Schultz said they ran into snags at first because the team tried to adapt elements of the plan to fit its needs, as opposed to adopting the whole strategy. "We found out that if you did it by the numbers, it works even better. But you had to take some giant leaps of faith that it would, in fact, work."[37]

American Standard workers are expected to assist each other to speed production, reduce costs and maintain high quality.

Working from a paper plan, managers had to move equipment often weighing 1,000 to 5,000 tons from different parts of the building so workers could flow product through one continuous cycle and eliminate waiting. That meant managers had to develop a companion plan that resembled a checkerboard because the equipment could not all be moved at once. "Some of the pieces needed different foundations, and we couldn't fall behind our production schedule, so we had to figure out how to maintain production and move the stuff at the same time."[38]

The cover story of *Chief Executive*, a magazine written by and for CEOs, summed up what Kampouris and his team had been able to achieve:

"Six years later, DFT has become the heart and soul of corporate culture at American Standard, and the courtly Kampouris becomes evangelical in describing how it has enabled inventory turns — the benchmark of plant efficiency American Standard uses for DFT — to increase from three times to nearly 11. Working capital has been reduced from 8.6 percent of sales to less than 5 percent — an impressive figure when compared with the average at U.S. companies: about 15 percent."[39]

In 1995, an assessment was made that showed the company was only taking advantage of about 50 percent of the benefits DFT offered. After the crisis had past, Kampouris was able to concentrate on DFT's real purpose — delivering on time by leveraging global capabilities. In the old days, a product in demand in one part of the world had to be supplied by the plant in that region. That meant sinking money into the facility so it could ramp up production for a particular demand. Meanwhile, a plant in another part of the world might be relatively idle. Under the DFT model, the idle plant should have the flexibility to fulfill the orders on time. "To satisfy local needs, all I have to do is import product from areas with excess capacity," Kampouris explained in 1998. "It's working as we speak today in the fixture business. You have to look at global sourcing to manage your capacities on a global basis."[40]

This requires facilities around the world to buy into the DFT process. Dave Gleditsch, a former JCIT executive who signed on with American

Standard full-time, developed a site certification plan. Gleditsch said plants must demonstrate a minimum of 15 average turns as a business unit and quick response to be DFT-certified.

"One of the supreme goals of DFT is to maximize the amount of product we make directly to order as opposed to having to guess into the future. That permits us to offer better response times to our customers than can our competitors. It permits us to manage with less inventory in finished goods, which lowers our cost."[31]

In fact, Kampouris' ultimate goal was to reduce working capital to zero, explained Joseph DeSantis, vice president of sales for the U.S. Plumbing Group. "We tell our customers they don't need a lot of inventory because we're doing that for them by having flexibility in our plants."[42]

Coaching the Team

In an interview, Kampouris described himself as a sort of coach for his management team. In turn, his senior executives have acted as assistant coaches for the rest of the organization. The team concept was one of the complementary effects DFT had on the corporation as the number of production stages was reduced. The team replaced the need for a supervisor at every level.

Wayne Jolliffe, vice president of human resources for the U.S. Plumbing Group, said employees from the top down became more responsible for their particular area. Jolliffe recalled how his boss, Eric Nutter, vice president and group executive of Americas Plumbing Products Group, fostered the team spirit by literally tearing down walls.

"We're office-less. When he arrived, he had us take down all the walls, and he sits right out in the middle with everybody else. As far as communication goes, things get done much faster because you don't have to walk around to find somebody. Now you can pretty much stand at your desk and see everybody working. It's sort of like a newsroom."[43]

As coach, the corporate headquarters built upon a business unit's skills by marrying them with

EMMANUEL KAMPOURIS

EMMANUEL KAMPOURIS STOOD BEFORE the 15 students who comprised the Unitary Products Group's first Leadership Development Class. He revealed no secrets on how to become a successful leader, because no such secrets exist. Strong character and unswerving integrity have been behind successful leaders from the beginning — which is precisely where Kampouris began his explanation.

Kampouris used the story of Joseph from the Old Testamant to illustrate the traits that keep an organization competitive during good times, resilient during down times, and ethical at all times. The story is just one example from the Bible, which Kampouris believes to be the best business book in history because it provides a road map for all aspects of life.

Sold into slavery by jealous brothers, Joseph relied on his abilities to triumph over adversity. He was brought to a position trust in Pharaoh's household by his integrity and honesty, never wavering from these two traits even as Pharaoh's wife tried to seduce him. Refusing to give in to temptation, Joseph was framed and thrown in prison. Joseph did not wallow in bitterness even though he was made to suffer for essentially holding to his morals. Instead, the qualities that resulted in his imprisonment elevated him in the eyes of those around him. Joseph soon ran the jailhouse. He eventually became the modern equivalent of a chief financial officer for Egypt. Joseph's conservative fiscal policy (he advised Pharaoh to put away 20 percent a year during prosperous times) brought wealth to Egypt and at the same time fed the famine-stricken people of other nations, including the very brothers who sold him into slavery in the first place.

Rising to the challenge has been one of Kampouris' hallmarks in his personal and professional life. He has been a natural athlete throughout his life, playing sports ranging from polo to golf (which he plays with an 11 handicap), and believes the key to success is to balance resilience on the one hand and competitiveness on the other. "Competitiveness is vital to win, but when the chips are down it is important to be more resilient, to stay focused and do the right thing."[1]

He does so by tapping an internal tuning fork of values. If someone lives a life by a code of ethics and integrity, the fork will ring the same way, no matter what type of decision has to be made. At American Standard, that means thinking beyond personal ambition for the good of the company, he said.

"The idea is to instill a sense of being part of a team that has ownership loyalty. We have that. The organization and the team of people are loyal to the company, with the sense that doing what is right for the company — and not what is right for the individual — is important."[2]

Kampouris considers himself as a coach, helping harness individual competitive spirits to function as a team, and developing the never-give-up attitude that is the hallmark of a historically successful company. As coach, he uses the Bible as his playbook. "There is a heart to the company," Kampouris said. "We have a legacy of trust, fairness, hard work, intelligence, wisdom and energy. The same legacy found in biblical principles."[3]

the methods of DFT and the practical knowledge needed to compete on a global scale. With senior vice presidents acting as mentors rather than supervisors, the term "empowerment" became more than just a corporate catchphrase, as the value of experienced managers and employees skyrocketed. Working as a team produced pride in the final outcome, as well as personal wealth for employees who were part of the ESOP. "We're really one of the few companies that have embraced these ideas," noted Senior Vice President Fred Allardyce. "It was quite dramatic to see that in a year's time, 40,000 employees were driving the business in a different way than they had been driving it as little as a year before."

"When you think about a large company, you wonder how a manager can influence what's going on. The fact of the matter is, he can, and he can quite significantly and quickly. Of course, we were facing a crisis of huge proportions, but even so it was interesting to see how quickly the whole corporation responded to the challenge, regardless of the language, regardless of where they were in the world."[44]

American Standard was emerging as a new company while it shifted back to production of its more traditional lines. In 1990, for example, the company sold the North American operations of its Railway Braking Products Division for $250 million. By the end of 1991, the company had divested Steelcraft, Fluid Power, Union Switch & Signal Company, Railway Braking and Tyler Refrigeration.[45]

As it concentrated on its core strengths, the company took an early lead in entering the emerging markets in Asia, particularly China. "China in the year 2000 is going to be the largest plumbing market in the world," Kampouris said. "It's humid and hot. They need sanitation. There's one loo on every floor, not every apartment."[46]

Although global operations were not new to American Standard, the way companies conducted business in a shrinking world was changing. On September 2, 1993, American Standard received the benefit of former Vice President Dan Quayle's experience when he was elected to the company's board of directors. While vice president under George Bush, Quayle headed the president's Council on Competitiveness, which focused on how well American industries competed in the worldwide marketplace. The company stated in a press release that "Mr. Quayle's election represents an important stage in the growth of American Standard." More than ever before, skills involving international government relations had become an evident need in the corporation as it negotiated business partnerships with national and local governments.[47]

Developing relations with the government of the People's Republic of China was of particular importance because that bustling nation has shown remarkable potential and resilience, especially in the face of the economic turmoil that rocked Asia in 1998. Gary Brogoch, vice president in charge of Plumbing Products for the Far East, remarked that China, with a population of 1.2 billion people, is still an untapped market.

The 1997-98 global economic downturn has not dampened the long-term promise of emerging Asian markets, but it underscored the need for foreign expertise.

Even its neighbors, suffering as they are from over-heated economies, still represent opportunity. "In 1985, we only had one joint venture in China, but by 1994 we entered into six new joint ventures. In much of Asia, the markets are new construction. As they mature, they will become more renovation-driven."[48]

By June 1994, American Standard had become the largest foreign producer of toilets and faucets in China. While visiting the successful plumbing fixture plant in Hua Mei, Senior Vice President George Kerckhove saw the vast potential in the nation's booming construction industry. Upon his return to New Jersey, Kerckhove recommended the commitment of $100 million to modernize or build more plants in China. "The board of directors was very supportive, except they said one thing — 'George, you don't have $100 million.'"[49]

So he and then-CFO Fred Allardyce journeyed to Hong Kong seeking investors and found seven or eight partners willing to invest about $10 million to $15 million each. American Standard's

board of directors agreed to put up the final $10 million. With the founding of a holding company, American Standard had its feet set firmly in Asia's fastest growing economy, which soon demanded improved comfort and safety as well as sanitation. By 1998, the number of joint ventures would grow to 11.

The pattern is a familiar and effective one in nations with emerging markets. As the standard of living rises in a country, sanitation is usually the first area to advance. American Standard lays the groundwork for better public health with the Plumbing Products Group. Soon human comfort and safety become issues, and American Standard can leverage its experience in these areas. Air

Below and above: American Standard moved quickly to become the largest producer of toilets and faucets in China, with 11 joint ventures, such as this manufacturing facility in Shanghai.

Conditioning Products in China, for example, has emerged as an integrated manufacturer and distributor of a broad range of residential and commercial air conditioning systems and related products. WABCO, too, has gained a manufacturing and distribution foothold in China with another joint enterprise.

In all, Plumbing Products, the most globally-oriented division of American Standard, has solid foundations in 24 nations and has most recently entered new markets in Eastern Europe, Spain and Portugal; Automotive Products sells in 17 nations; and Air Conditioning Products manufac-

tures in 10 nations, including the United States, with a recent enterprise established in Australia.

Above: A showroom in Shanghai. Because the nation is still developing, the market in China is mostly new construction.

Right: By 1998, Air Conditioning Products had training centers and manufacturing operations established in 10 nations.

Going Public Again

Managers and workers together engineered a remarkable turnaround. In February 1995, American Standard once again became a publicly traded company, organized as American Standard Companies, Inc., under which operate the various companies comprising the corporation. "The February IPO was made possible by our employees' successful transformation of American Standard into a world leader in Demand Flow Technology," Kampouris told an audience of mostly employees. "This outstanding effort and achievement has given your company a distinct competitive edge and enhanced growth prospects."[50]

The IPO was one of the largest sales completed by a company that had been taken over in the 1980s. The IPO raised $290 million with the sale of 14.5 million shares at $20 a share. The money was used to pay down debt accrued when American Standard borrowed $325 million to redeem high-interest bonds.[51]

Kampouris described 1995 as a "watershed" year for American Standard. "We completed our first year back in the public arena. Consolidated sales and operating income rose to record levels as we continued to build the solid foundation necessary to achieve our stated corporate performance goals for our existing businesses: 15 inventory turns, 15 percent operating margin and zero working capital."[52] Income for 1995 reached $142 million or $1.90 per share — American Standard's first positive gain since the LBO. Revenue reached $5.2 billion.[53]

The following year was even better. Revenues hit another all-time high of $5.8 billion with earnings per share increasing 27 percent. That year Kelso & Company sold its 20.8 million shares (about 27 percent of the company) for about $780 million.[54]

Medical Systems

On March 10, 1997, American Standard announced the planned acquisition of the European medical diagnostics business Sorin Biomedica S.p.A., an affiliate of Fiat Group. That same day it announced plans to merge with INCSTAR Corporation, another medical diagnostics company based in Stillwater, Minnesota.[55] These companies and two others formed the Medical Systems Group, the company's fourth business sector.

American Standard entered the medical field when investments it had made in certain areas showed commercial promise. "Our initial investments are a function of the entrepreneurial spirit of our chairman," noted Fred Allardyce. "It was his spirit and the support we had from Kelso that enabled us to make these kinds of wild-card investments. They turned out to have commercial viability and became intriguing prospects for American Standard to pursue."[56]

Some of the early investments in the medical field came about almost by accident. In 1992, Kampouris visited a laser laboratory at Rutgers University run by Dr. Daniel Murnick, who was developing a laser to close small cracks in ceramic products that sometimes occur during the kiln process. The laser could eliminate the need to run product through the kiln again, saving time and electricity.

While checking on the laser's progress, Kampouris noticed a smaller laser, which Murnick said was designed to measure global warming. He told Kampouris that his wife was a medical physicist and had discovered another use for the atmospheric laser. Dr. Janet Murnick was adapting the laser, called LARA (Laser Assisted Ratio Analyzer), to measure exhaled breath as an early diagnostic tool for illnesses related to the gastrointestinal system. "There's a lot of information in the breath," Janet Murnick explained.

"There's a lot you can look at, like liver disorders, ulcers, gastric cancer. You can get information on people who don't digest properly. The laser can be used for the initial diagnosis, and if the patient is treated, do follow-up tests to see if the cure has occurred."[57]

Intrigued by the explanation, Kampouris had his office call Janet Murnick several days later, and eventually they agreed on an investment. Murnick, who has since become a vice president at American Standard, formed the company Alimenterics. The laser received EMA (Europe's continental medical agency) approval in 1998. It is already being sold in Canada and Europe.

Sienna Biotech, Inc., adapted lasers in a similar way. Using a proprietary new technology it called Copalis (Coupled Particle Light Scattering), the company was able to perform multiple tests on a single blood sample.[58] Its first products, which focus on discovering prenatal congenital diseases, received clearance from the FDA in 1996, and applications for a broad range of diseases are being developed, noted Dr. Judy Britz.

"American Standard's philosophy centers on Demand Flow Technology, and I think that the types of technology American Standard has invested in lend themselves to a demand flow philosophy for patient management in health care."[59]

Vice President of Special Projects Luigi Gandini said the company's involvement in the medical business "is an indication that the corporation is vital and modern. We're not sitting down and waiting for things to happen."[60] The future for this new endeavor is still wide open. Kampouris said the objective, naturally, is to create value for the stockholder. How American Standard does this remains to be seen.

"Whether we spin them off or grow them will depend on how well we manage the process. It's exciting. It's got so much interesting opportunity because these businesses are recession-proof. If you have good technology and can carve out a niche, recessions don't mean very much because

Above: An air-actuated disc brake, an example of Westinghouse's revolutionary antilock braking system.

Opposite page: Copalis was designed to perform multiple tests simultaneously on a single test sample.

people need good medical equipment, and that has nothing to do with the Dow Jones, up or down."[51]

Advances in technologies aren't limited to medical systems. WABCO introduced electronic braking, for instance, which evolved from its antilock braking system (ABS). Engineers had been working on electronic braking for 10 years, and the system quickly became standard equipment on trucks operated by the world's largest truck manufacturer, Mercedes-Benz. Vice Chairman Horst Hinrichs, formerly senior vice president of the WABCO Automotive Products Group, said the sector is still relatively small when compared to competitors, but the combination of innovation and globalization will increase it. "We are going away from components to thinking in terms of systems," he said. "Our objective has to be in the longer term to become a much more sizable player in the industry."[62]

Air Conditioning Products launched a major initiative in the 1990s to develop a minisplit system, which is essentially a ductless room air conditioning system consisting of two separate units, and has

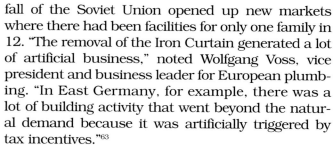

Above and below left: Selling under the Trane and American Standard brand names gives the corporation two bites from the same apple.

Below right: Electronic stability control provides shorter stopping distance and increased braking stability, and at the same time the system also monitors the performance reserves of the wheel brakes.

fall of the Soviet Union opened up new markets where there had been facilities for only one family in 12. "The removal of the Iron Curtain generated a lot of artificial business," noted Wolfgang Voss, vice president and business leader for European plumbing. "In East Germany, for example, there was a lot of building activity that went beyond the natural demand because it was artificially triggered by tax incentives."[63]

Although recession in many parts of Europe has dampened the market, conditions will likely improve as economies and monetary units integrate. American Standard is preparing by investing in former communist nations, such as Bulgaria, where the cost of doing business is lower. "We've built two plants for fixtures and faucets there," noted Wilfried Delker, vice president and business leader of Worldwide Fittings. "It takes time to train people and get them into our mentality and level of quality, but it will be important for the future."[64]

Diversified with a Common Goal

The meltdown of Asian economies – with the notable exception of China — put American Standard's strength in sharp relief. The company achieved a record $6 billion in sales in 1997. "Our

since gone into worldwide distribution. In 1998 the sector was reorganized into three separate businesses: Worldwide Applied Systems, headed by James Schultz; North American Unitary, headed by David Pannier; and International Unitary Products, led by Bruce Achenbach.

Plumbing fixtures and fittings remain American Standard's most traditional line. Worldwide, it sells under the American Standard, Ideal Standard, Porcher, Absolute and Sottini brand names. Company leaders expect growth in this area as the global economy improves the standard of living for people around the world. In Eastern Europe, for example, the

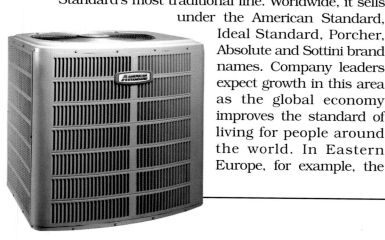

Plumbing fixtures remain American Standard's most traditional line, and the one for which it is famous.

ability to partially overcome these adversities clearly validates our strategies built on our global diversity and leadership positions worldwide, which provide the foundation for strong sales and earnings growth," Kampouris wrote to stockholders.[65]

With employees holding a major stake in the company, Kampouris is on target with a goal of $10 billion in sales and zero working capital. With the approach of the new millennium, American Standard is searching for a slogan or motto that defines its diverse businesses, an organization that succeeds. Although several have been considered, the theme, "Your Well-Being is Our Business" strikes the right chords because throughout its history, its businesses have revolved around the improvement of lives.

A man inspired by the Old Testament, Kampouris wants to maintain an organization that succeeds but stays "humble and upholds standards. One that has wisdom and that does right. And by the year 2000, I'd like to have created at least a thousand new millionaires among our associates."[66]

NOTES TO SOURCES

Chapter One

1. *Cooperation*, Vol. No. II, January-February 1929.
2. *Cooperation*, Vol. II, January-February, 1902. American Radiator & Standard Sanitary publication: p. 2.
3. *Ibid.*: p. 3.
4. *Ibid.*
5. *Ibid.*
6. *Ibid.*
7. "Heating Man," *Fortune* magazine, April 1935: p. 161.
8. Clarence Woolley's correspondence to American Radiator, date unknown: p. 1.
9. "Heating Man," *Fortune* magazine: p. 161.
10. Woolley correspondence: p. 1-2.
11. Milton Moskowitz, Robert Levering and Michael Katz, *Everybody's Business*, Bantam Doubleday, New York, NY.: p. 125.
12. 1903 American Radiator annual report.
13. 1904 company advertisement.
14. 1907 American Radiator annual report.
15. *Ibid.*
16. Woolley correspondence, September 18, 1914.
17. 1918 American Radiator Company annual report: pp. 6, 10.

18. *Ibid.*: p 5.
19. Daniel Yergin, *The Prize*, Simon & Shuster, New York, NY, 1991: p. 178.
20. 1919 American Radiator Company annual report: p. 8.
21. 1921 American Radiator Company annual report: p. 16.
22. *Fortune* magazine, April, 1935: p. 188.
23. Ed Wencek, *The History and Origin of American Standard, Inc.*, unpublished manuscript, 1993: p. 50.
24. 1921 American Radiator Company annual report: p. 16.
25. *Fortune* magazine, April, 1935: p. 188.

Chapter One Sidebar: Joseph Bond

1. *Cooperation*, Vol. No. II, January-February 1929.
2. *Ibid.*
3. *Ibid.*
4. *Ibid.*

Chapter One Sidebar: Radiator Building

1. *The New York Times*, February 20, 1994, section 10: p. 7.
2. "Headquarters Building Restoration Underway," *Standard Bearer*, Vol. 8, No. 3, 1974: p. 5.

3. "Headquarters Building Restoration Underway," *Standard Bearer*, Vol. 8, No. 3, 1974: p. 5.
4. *Wall Street Journal*, Sept. 1, 1988: p. 2.
5. Michael Moskowitz, Robert Levering and Michael Katz, *Everybody's Business*, Doubleday, New York, NY, 1990: p. 124.
6. *New York Magazine*, Dec. 27, 1982-Jan. 3, 1983: p. 32.

Chapter Two

1. *Theodore Ahrens — A Tribute*, by Vic Calver, of the staff of the Southern Plumber, date unknown.
2. John Duffy, *The Sanitarians, A History of American Public Health*, Board of Trustees of the University of Illinois, 1990: p. 7.
3. The New Encyclopaedia Britannica, Macropaedia, 15th Edition, Vol. 23, 1997: p. 803.
4. John Duffy, *The Sanitarians, A History of American Public Health*: p. 7.
5. "Cholera," *Microsoft Encarta 97 Encyclopedia*, Microsoft Corporation, 1993-1996.

6. "Thomas Crapper: Myth & Reality," *Plumbing & Mechanical Magazine*, June 1993: http://www.theplumber.com/crapper.html.
7. "The Men That Made the Water Closet," *Plumbing & Mechanical Magazine*, June 1993: http://www.theplumber.com/crapper.html.
8. "The Housewares Story," by Earl Lifshey, National Housewares Manufacturer's Association: p. 202.
9. *Baths*, 1890 Standard Manufacturing catalog: p. 1.
10. American Radiator & Standard Sanitary Corporation, History of the Corporation, date and author unknown.
11. *Baths*, 1890 Standard manufacturing catalog: p. 1.
12. *Cooperation*, American Radiator & Standard Sanitary Corporation, Vol. II January-February 1933: pp. 1-2.
13. *Ibid*.
14. Company biography on Theodore Ahrens, date and author unknown. Company archives.
15. "American Radiator & Standard Sanitary Corporation," *Fortune* magazine, April 1940: p. 157.
16. "American Radiator & Standard Sanitary Corp.," *Fortune* magazine, March 1940: p. 157.

17. Company biography on Theodore Ahrens. date and author unknown. Company archives.
18. Mark Sullivan, *Our Times*, abridged version, ed. by Dan Rather (Scribner) 1996: p. 185.
19. "Porcelain enamelling," *Encyclopaedia Britannica*, Vo. 9, Micropaedia Ready Reference, 1998: p. 613.
20. Theodore Ahrens, "The Plumber in Our Industry," company files, Feb. 2, 1929: p. 3.
21. "American Radiator & Standard Sanitary Corp." *Fortune* magazine, March 1940: pp. 158, 157.
22. "Color and Style in Bathroom Furnishing and Decoration, Standard Plumbing Fixtures," Standard Sanitary Manufacturing Company catalog, 1929, American Standard archives: p. 3.
23. *Ibid*.

Chapter Three

1. "Heating Man," *Fortune* magazine, April 1935: p. 81.
2. *Fortune* magazine: p. 164.
3. *The New York Times*, Dec. 15, 1928; Dec. 29, 1928.
4. 1928 American Radiator annual report: p. 10.
5. "A Study of American Radiator Company and Standard Sanitary

Manufacturing Company and Their Merger," Manowitch Brothers investment report, May 27, 1929.
6. "Heating Man," *Fortune*: p. 59.
7. American Radiator & Sanitary Corporation, "History of the Corporation," unpublished history, date and author unknown: p. 8.
8. Manowitch Brothers study, May 27, 1929.
9. 1929 AR&SS annual report, 1929: p. 2.
10, *Ibid*.
11. *Ibid*.
12. 1934 AR&SS annual report.
13. "Heating Man," *Fortune* magazine.
14. Sally Jacobs, "Everybody Loses," *New England Business*, May 6, 1985: p. 88.
15. 1930 AR&SS annual report.
16. *The New York Times*, December 25, 1935.
17. 1932 AR&SS annual report: p.4.
18. Alan Axelrod and Charles Phillips, *What Every American Should Know About American History*, Bob Adams Publishers, Holbrook, Massachusetts, 1992: p. 277.
19. "Heating Man," *Fortune*, April, 1935.
20. *The New York Times*, April 13, 1933: p. 31.
21. *The New York Times*, May 3, 1933: p. 31.

22. *Illinois Master Plumber*, March, 1934.
23. "The Bathtub Shortage," *The Plumbing News*, Vol. 36, No. 13, Standard Sanitary Manufacturing Company magazine, May 1934.
24. "Heating Man," *Fortune*: p. 81.
25. *Ibid.*
26. *Ibid.*
27. *The New York Times*, April 11, 1935: p. 39.
28. Annabelle Christie, interviewed by the author September 8, 1997. Transcript: pp. 1, 4-5.
29. 1933 AR&SS annual report: p.1.
30. "Heating Man," *Fortune*: p. 164.
31. Ed Wencek, *The History and Origin of American Standard, Inc.*, unpublished manuscript, 1993.
32. "Heating Man," *Fortune:* p. 164.
33. Jonathon Martin, "American Standard, Inc.," *International Directory of Company Histories*, Volume II, St. James Press, Chicago, 1990: p. 663.
34. "American Radiator & Standard Sanitary Corp., *Fortune*, March 1940: p. 157.
35. *Ibid.*
36. Letter from Clarence Woolley to AR&SS shareholders, dated September 25, 1936.
37. *Fortune*, March 1940: p. 158.

38. *Ibid.*
39. *Fortune* magazine, March 1940: p. 159.
40. *Ibid*: p.160.
41. *Fortune*: p. 156.

Chapter Three Sidebar: Henry Reed

1. Bill Stern, KRDA, National Broadcasting Company, September, 1947.
2. *Ibid.*

Chapter Three Sidebar: Clarence Woolley

1. Commencement address to Colgate University granduates, June, 1928.
2. "Heating Man," *Fortune*, April 1935: p.188.
3. Clarence Woolley, Obituary, *Santa Ana Register*, Santa Ana, California, July 20, 1956.

Chapter Four

1. "War Production Has the Call," AR&SS advertisement, October 1943.
2. 1940 AR&SS annual report: pp.2-3.
3. Annual Report, 1940: p. 5.
4. *Ibid.*
5. John Crider, *The New York Times*, January 2, 1940: p. 1.
6. 1940 AR&SS annual report: p. 5.
7. "Priorities and the Home," *The New York Times* Sunday supplement,

November 22, 1942, p. 4D.
8. 1941 AR&SS annual report: p. 2.
9. "War Production Has the Call," AR&SS advertisement, October 1943.
10. Federal-Mogul Lines Special Issue, September 1944.
11. Edward Wencek, *History of American Standard*, unpublished manuscript, date unknown.
12. 1942 annual report: p. 4.
13. 1941 annual report: p. 4.
14. Colin Wise, interviewed by Catherine Lackner, April 1, 1998. Transcript: p. 17.
15 Michael Evamy, *The First 100 Years: Ideal Standard*, Ideal Standard, 1996: pp. 24-25.
16 1944 annual report: p. 5.
17. George Tindall, David Shi, *America*, W.W. Norton & Company, New York, 1989: p. 791.
18. 1945 annual report: p. 3.
19. *History of the Corporation*, American Radiator & Standard Sanitary Corporation, brief history outline: p. 7.
20. 1945 annual report: p. 5.
21. George Tindall, David Shi, *America*: p. 791.

Chapter Five

1. 1949 AR&SS annual report: p. 5.
2. George Tindall and David Shi, *America*, W.W.

Norton & Company, New York, 1989: p. 790.
3. *The New York Times*, April 27, 1946: p. 10.
4. 1946 annual report: p. 3.
5. *Ibid.*: p. 3.
6. 1945 annual report: p. 4.
7. 1947 annual report: p. 8.
8. 1946 annual report: pp. 6-7.
9. *Ibid.*: p. 6.
10. *Ibid.*: pp. 6-7.
11. 1947 annual report: p.10.
12. *Ibid.*: p. 10.
13. *The New York Times*, March 1, 1948: p. 9.
14. 1949 annual report: p.1.
15. David Halberstam, *The Fifties*, Ballantine Books, New York, 1993: p. 134.
16. *Ibid.*
17. *The New York Times*, January 4, 1949: p. 32.
18. 1949 annual report: p. 5.
19. 1950 annual report: pp. 3-4.

Chapter Six

1. *Fortune* magazine, June 1954: p. 134.
2. David Halberstam, *The Fifties*, Ballantine Books, New York, 1993: p. 75.
3. *The Wall Street Journal*, June 7, 1951.
4. "All the Way Into the Kitchen," *Business Week*, September 15, 1951: p. 77.
5. 1951 American-Standard annual report: p. 4.
6. *Business Week*, September 15, 1951: p. 77.

7. David Halberstam, *The Fifties*, Ballantine Books, New York, 1993: p. 142.
8. *Business Week*, Sept. 15, 1951: pp. 77-78.
9. 1956 American-Standard annual report: p. 24.
10. *Ibid.*: p. 12.
11. Frank Berberich, interviewed by Catherine Lackner, March 19, 1998. Transcript: p. 4.
12. 1952 annual report: p. 4.
13. American-Standard press release, release, April 2, 1950.
14. *Ibid.*
15. *Fortune* magazine, June 1954: p.134.
16. Fred Jaqua, interviewed by the author, September 9, 1997. Transcript: pp. 2-3.
17. 1954 annual report: p. 4.
18. Remarks made by Joseph Grazier at an employee dinner held in Louisville, November 4, 1954.
19. *Fortune* magazine, June 1954: p. 134.
20. Grazier remarks from Louisville employee dinner, November 4, 1953.
21. *Ibid.*
22. Henry Steiner, interviewed by the author, November 21, 1997. Transcript: p. 8.
23. 1957 annual report: p. 7.
24. 1956 annual report: p. 5.
25. Don Feigel, interviewed by the author, November

21, 1997. Transcript: p. 6.
26. Colin Wise, interviewed by Catherine Lackner, April 1, 1998. Transcript: p. 27.
27. Italian newspaper, *Giornale Di Brescia*, July 1, 1958: p. 5.
28. *Ibid.*
29. 1959 annual report: p. 3.

Chapter Six Sidebar: Biography of Theodore Mueller

1. From company biography and press releases, authors unknown.
2. From news clip, source unknown, September 24, 1957.
3. *The Pittsburgh Post-Gazette*, September 24, 1957.
4. From news clip, source unknown, September 24, 1957.

Chapter Seven

1. *Fortune*, April 15, 1967.
2. American-Standard advertisement appearing in *Better Homes and Gardens*, May 1960.
3. *Better Homes and Gardens*, August 1960.
4. *The New York Times*, September 21, 1960: p. 51.
5. *Ibid.*
6. David De Wahl, interviewed by Catherine Lackner March 17, 1998. Transcript: p. 2.
7. De Wahl interview, transcript: p. 5.

8. 1960 American Standard annual report: p. 2.
9. *The New York Times*, January 14, 1963: p. 1.
10. *The New York Times*, September 5, 1963: p. 39.
11. *Ibid.*
12. *Ibid.*
13. Fred Jaqua, interviewed by the author September 9, 1997. Transcript: p. 5.
14. 1963 annual report.
15. 1965 annual report.
16. Alexander Apostolopoulos, interviewed by Catherine Lackner, March 18, 1998. Transcript: p. 4.
17. *Fortune*, April 15, 1967.
18. "So Near, So Far," *Forbes*, April 15, 1967.
19. David De Wahl, interviewed by Catherine Lackner, March 17, 1998. Transcript: p. 6-7.
20. Fred Jaqua, interviewed by the author, September 9, 1997. Transcript: p. 2-3.
21. Herbert Hadley, interviewed by Catherine Lackner, March 30, 1998. Transcript: p. 2.
22. Hugh Hoffman, interviewed by Catherine Lackner, March 30, 1998. Transcript: p. 3.
23. John Grant, interviewed by Catherine Lackner, March 17, 1998. Transcript: p. 1.
24. 1966 American Standard annual report, p. 1.
25. Carl Zeigler, interviewed by the author, November 21, 1997. Transcript: p. 5.
26. David De Wahl, interviewed by Catherine Lackner, March 17, 1998. Transcript: p. 6.
27. John Donnelly, interviewed by Catherine Lackner, March 27, 1998. Transcript: p. 3.
28. *Ibid.*: p. 6-7.
29. *Ibid.*: p. 3.
30. "American Bathroom Rated Low in Study," *The New York Times*, May 9, 1966: p. 1.
31. 1966 annual report, p. 7.
32. *The New York Times*, May 11, 1967: p. 68.
33. *The Wall Street Journal*, June 2, 1967: p. 2.
34. *The New York Times*, May 12, 1967: p. 67.
35. *The Wall Street Journal*, May 15, 1967: p. 23.
36. *Mpulse*, inhouse publication of the Mosler Safe Company, March 1973: p. 7.
37. *Ibid.*: p. 19.
38. Jaqua interview, transcript: p. 4.
39. William Marquard, interviewed by the author, March 25, 1998. Transcript: p. 5.
40. *The Wall Street Journal*, May 9, 1968: p. 21.
41. Horst Hinrichs, interviewed by the author, November 21, 1997. Transcript: p. 4.
42. *The Wall Street Journal*, June 4, 1968: p. 8.
43. G. Eric Nutter, interviewed by the author, November 20, 1997. Transcript: p. 1.
44. American-Standard press release, June 5, 1969.
45. Alan Root, interviewed by Catherine Lackner, March 26, 1998. Transcript: p. 7.
46. *Forbes*, February 20, 1978, pp. 86-87.
47. Robert Crooks, interviewed by Catherine Lackner, March 31, 1998. Transcript: p. 11.
48. *Fortune*, April 15, 1967.

Chapter Seven Sidebar: Mosler Safes

1. *Mpulse*, inhouse publication of the Mosler Safe Company, March 1973: p. 31.
2. *Ibid.*: p. 13.

Chapter Seven Sidebar: Phil Donohue Show

1. "Dayton TV show Topples Toilet Taboo!" *Action Report*, Vol. 1, No. 3, October 1968: pp. 1-2.
2 *Ibid.*

Chapter Eight

1. *The New York Times*, March 13, 1914, editorial section: p. 8.
2. *Ibid.*
3. Westinghouse Air Brake, 75th Anniversary, Wilmerding, Pennsylvania, 1944: pp. 1-5.
4. L.K. Sillcox, *Safety In Early American Railway*

Operation 1853-1871, 1936, Princeton University Press: p.18.

5. *Brake-Ways, Seventy-Five Years Westinghouse* WABCO, Hanover, Germany: p. 5.

6. Westinghouse Air Brake Company, 75th Anniversary, Wilmerding, Pa.: p.4.

7. *Brake-Ways, 75 Years Westinghouse Hanover, 1884-1959*, from American Standard archives.

8. Westinghouse Airbrake Company, 75th Anniversary: p.9.

9. *Brake-Ways, 75 Years Westinghouse Hanover, 1884-1959*.

10. Edgar A. Haine, *Railroad Wrecks*, Corwall Books, 1908, Rosemont Publishing & Printing Corp., 1993, New York: p.17.

11. *The New York Times*, March 3, 1914: p. 3.

12. *Ibid.*

13. *Ibid.*

14. *Ibid.*: p. 8.

15. Encyclopedia Brittanica, volume 12, 15th edition: p. 606.

16. *The New York Times*: pp. 3, 8.

17. *Brake-Ways*, 1959: p. 10.

18. Letter to the editor appearing in *The New York Times*, June 1, 1973, Letter to the Editor.

19. Westinghouse Air Brake Company, 75th Anniversary: p. 12.

20. L.K. Sillcox, *Safety in Early American Railway Operation 1853-1871*, pp. 18-19.

21. Thomas C. Cochran, *Railroad Leaders 1845-1890*, Harvard University Press, Cambridge, Mass., 1953, pp. 27-28, 206.

22. Edgar A. Haine, *Railroad Wrecks*: p. 17.

23. Westinghouse Air Brake, 75th Anniversary: p. 12.

24. Edgar Haine, *Railroad Wrecks*: p. 17.

25. Enclyclopedia Brittanica, volume 12, 15th edition: p. 605.

26. Westinghouse Air Brake, 75th Anniversary: pp. 17, 57.

27. 75th Anniversary: pp. 45-46.

28. *History of American Standard*, compiled by retired employee Ed Wencek throughout his career.

29. The *Wall Street Journal*, June 29, 1955: p. 1.

30. *Ibid.*

31. *The Wall Street Journal*, December 2, 1988: p. 12.

32. *The Wall Street Journal*, January 24, 1955: p. 10.

33. *The Wall Street Journal*, October 14, 1959: p. 6.

34. Giancarlo Aimetti, interviewed by Catherine Lackner, April 1, 1998. Transcript: p. 5-9.

35. *Ibid.*

36. Horst Hinrichs, interviewed by Alex Lieber, December 21, 1998, by telephone.

37. Eric Reinecke, interviewed by the author, March 31, 1998, transcript: p. 4.

38. Hinrichs interview, by telephone.

39. Aimetti interview, transcript: p. 5.

Chapter Nine

1. William Marquard, interviewed by the author, March 25, 1998. Transcript: p. 7.

2. American Standard annual report, 1970: p. 3.

3. Adrien Deshotel, interviewed by the author, March 25, 1998. Transcript: p. 7.

4. Sandy McGregor, interviewed by the author, March 30, 1998. Transcript: p. 6.

5. John Grant, interviewed by Catherine Lacker, March 17, 1998. Transcript: p. 2.

6. Barbara Glenn, interviewed by Catherine Lackner, March 31, 1998. Transcript: p. 2.

7. William Marquard, interviewed by the author, March 25, 1998. Transcript: p. 7.

8. *Standard Bearer*, "Marquard is Named Chief Executive," Vol. 5, No.4, September-October 1971: p. 1.

9. John Geer, interviewed by Catherine Lackner,

March 24, 1998. Transcript: p. 3.

10. Marquard interview, transcript: p. 10.

11. David De Wahl, interviewed by Catherine Lackner March 17, 1998. Transcript: p. 7.

12. Alan Root, interviewed by Catherine Lackner, March 26, 1998. Transcript: p. 4.

13. Angela Tripoti, interviewed by Catherine Lackner, March 25, 1998. Transcript: p. 5.

14. Hans Zinzow, interviewed by Catherine Lackner. Transcript: p. 3.

15. American Standard 1971 annual report: p. 3.

16. Robert Levinson, interviewed by Catherine Lackner, March 19, 1998. Transcript: pp. 3, 11.

17. Henry Steiner, interviewed by the author November 21, 1997. Transcript: p. 4-6.

18. *Standard Bearer*, Vol. 6, No. 4, Fall Issue, 1972.

19. *Standard Bearer*, Vol. 8, No. 1, Winter 1973.

20. *Standard Bearer*, Vol. 8, No. 1, Winter 1974.

21. *Standard Bearer*, Vol. 7, No. 1, Winter Issue 1973.

22. Roy Satchell, interviewed by Catherine Lackner March 24, 1998. Transcript: p. 2.

23. 1975 American Standard annual report: p. 2.

24. "American Standard Inc. Adopts LIFO Method For All Its Operations," *The Wall Street Journal*, January 7, 1975: p. 33.

25. "Putting Humpty Dumpty Together Again," *Forbes*, February 20, 1978.

26. Roy Satchell, interviewed by Catherine Lackner, March 24, 1998. Transcript: pp. 5-6.

27. Cyril Gallimore, interviewed by Catherine Lackner, April 2, 1998. Transcript: p. 13.

28. Roy Satchell, interviewed by Catherine Lackner, March 24, 1998. Transcript: pp. 5-6.

29. *Ibid.*

30. *Ibid.*, p 9.

31. *Barron's*, "American Standard Broader — Mix Pays Off," September 19, 1977.

32. *Forbes*, February 20, 1978: p. 87.

33. *Ibid.*

34. "Rise of Orders for Rail Equipment May Ease But Red Flag Isn't Being Raised on Stocks," *The Wall Street Journal*, February 20, 1979: p. 41.

35. American Standard press release, October 25, 1979: p. 2.

36. 1979 annual report.

Chapter Ten

1. "Happy Days at American Standard," *Fortune*, September 22, 1980.

2. *Ibid.*

3. "The Five Best-Managed Companies," *Dun's Review*, December 1980.

4. "A Matter of Labels," *Forbes*, May 12, 1980: p. 159.

5. *Ibid.*

6. 1980 American Standard annual report.

7. *The New York Times*, July 9, 1980.

8. American Standard press release, December 8, 1980.

9. 1981 annual report: p. 5.

10. *Financial World*, 1981.

11. 1982 annual report: p. 2.

12. *Modern Industrial Energy*, July 1981: pp. 13-14.

13. Bill Marquard, interviewed by the author, March 25, 1998. Transcript: p. 12.

14. "After Pet Takeover, IC Industries is Set for New Conquests," *The New York Times*, June 22, 1982, Section D: p. 5.

15. "Trane Files Suit To Block IC Move," *The New York Times*, November 19, 1983, Section 1: p. 34.

16. William Klug, interviewed by the author September 19, 1997. Transcript: p. 9.

17. George Kerckhove, interviewed by the author, November 20, 1997. Transcript: p. 17.

18. Bill Marquard, interviewed by the author,

March 25, 1998. Transcript: p. 14.

19. *Ibid.*
20. David Pannier, interviewed by Alex Lieber, April 14, 1998. Transcript: p. 6.
21. Kerckhove interview, transcript: pp. 10-11.
22. Klug interview, transcript: p. 9.
23. James Schultz, interviewed by Alex Lieber April 14, 1998. Transcript: p. 2.
24. 1984 annual report: p. 2.
25. 1985 annual report: p. 2.
26. Benson Stein, interviewed by Catherine Lackner, March 18, 1998. Transcript: p. 2.
27. Frank Nickell, interviewed by Catherine Lackner April 6, 1998. Transcript: p. 2.
28. 1986 American Standard annual report: p. 2.
29. 1985 annual report: p. 4.
30. Alan Root, interviewed by the author, March 26, 1998. Transcript: p. 8.

Chapter Eleven

1. Trane 1938 Trane annual report: p. 5.
2. Art Scheskie, *A Brief History of Trane*, The Trane Company. This history is continually updated on Trane's web page at http://www.trane.com.

3. *Ibid.*
4. George Kerckhove, *The History of Trane, 1913-1997*, unpublished manuscript, p. 2. Mr. Kerckhove kindly and efficiently summarized Trane's annual reports for use in this book.
5. *Ibid.*
6. Scheskie, *A Brief History of Trane.*
7. Kerckhove, *The History of Trane*: p. 2.
8. Scheskie, *A Brief History of Trane.*
9. 1938 Trane annual report: p. 4.
10. 1938 Trane annual report: p. 5.
11. Scheskie.
12. 1941 Trane annual report: p. 7.
13. Kerckhove: p. 4.
14. *Ibid.*: p. 2.
15. 1962 Trane annual report: p. 5.
16. Kerckhove: p. 24.
17. *Ibid.*: p. 26.
18. 1973 Trane annual report: p. 4.
19. Scheskie.
20. Robert Metz, "Trane's Deal For G.E. Unit," *The New York Times*, Section D: p. 10.

Chapter Twelve

1. "The Man Who Puts Working Capital To Work," *Chief Executive*, October 1996.
2. "Black & Decker commences cash tender offer for American

Standard," *Business Wire*, January 27, 1988.
3. Joseph Weber and Laurie Baum, "Black & Decker Sees 'A Perfect Fit,'" *Business Week*, McGraw Hill, February 8, 1998: p. 27.
4. *Ibid.*
5. Adrian Deshotel, interviewed by the author March 25, 1998. Transcript: p. 13.
6. Benson Stein, interviewed by Catherine Lackner, March 18, 1998. Transcript: p. 3.
7. Paula Schnorbus, "B&D Turns On the Power," Information Access Company, Decisions Publishing Inc., Marketing & Media Decisions, May 1988.
8. *Ibid.*
9. Weber and Baum, "Black & Decker Sees 'A Perfect Fit,'" *Business Week*: p. 27.
10. Robert Wellbrock, interviewed by Catherine Lackner, March 31, 1998. Transcript: p. 4.
11. *The Wall Street Journal*, February 2, 1988: p. 43.
12. "American Standard rejects Unsolicited Takeover Bid," PR Newswire, February 9, 1988.
13. Robert Cole, "Decker Tops Standard's New Offer," *The New York Times*, March 5, 1988: p. 35.
14. Angela Tripodi, interviewed by Catherine

Lackner, March 25, 1998. Transcript: p. 8.

15. "Black & Decker Says Barriers Must Go," PR Newswire, March 11, 1988.

16. Brad Rudin, "Court decision foils 'paracute,'" *Pension & Investment Age*, Crain Communications, Inc., April 18, 1988: p. 6.

17. Daniel F. Cuff, "Kelso Chairman Holds No Love for Wall Street," *The New York Times*, March 24, 1988: p. 5.

18. Frank Nickell, interviewed by Catherine Lackner, April 6, 1998. Transcript: pp. 5-6.

19. Robert Cole, "Standard Endorses Kelso Bid," *The New York Times*, March 18, 1988: Section D, p. 1.

20. Louis O. Kelso and Patricia Hetter Kelso, *Democracy and Economic Power: Extending the ESOP Revolution*, Ballinger Publishing Company, Cambridge, Mass., 1986: pp. 52-53.

21. *The Wall Street Journal*, March 21, 1988: p. 6.

22. John Geer, interviewed by Catherine Lackner, March 24, 1998. Transcript: p. 7.

23. *The Wall Street Journal*, March 23, 1988.

24. Henry Steiner, interviewed by the author, November 21, 1997. Transcript: p. 9.

25. Raymond Pipes, interviewed by Catherine Lackner March 27, 1998. Transcript: p. 5-6.

26. William Marquard, interviewed by the author, March 25, 1998. Transcript: p. 21.

27. Fred Jaqua, interviewed by the author, September 9, 1997. Transcript: pp. 13-14.

28. Shawn Tully, "Prophet of Zero Working Capital," reprinted through the courtesy of *Fortune* by *Time* Inc., 1994.

29. Jennifer Reingold and John Kimelman, "Nerves of Steel," *Financial World*, May 23, 1995: p. 31.

30. James Schultz, interviewed by Alex Lieber, April 14, 1998. Transcript: p. 5.

31. Dave Pannier, interviewed by the author, April 14, 1998. Transcript: pp. 16-17.

32. John Costanza, interviewed by Alex Lieber, April 13, 1998. Transcript: p. 15.

33. Emmanuel Kampouris, interviewed by the author, August 10, 1998. Transcript: p. 8.

34. Cyril Gallimore, interviewed by Catherine Lackner, April 2, 1998. Transcript: p. 5.

35. *Chief Executive*, October 1996.

36. James Schultz, interviewed by Alex Lieber, April 14, 1998. Transcript: p. 5.

37. *Ibid.*

38. *Ibid.*

39. *Ibid.*: p. 7.

40. *Chief Executive*, October 1996.

41. Kampouris interview, transcript: p. 8.

42. David Gleditsch, interviewed by Catherine Lackner, April 7, 1998. Transcript: p. 3.

42. Joseph DeSantis, interviewed by Catherine Lackner, March 24, 1998. Transcript: p. 7.

43. Wayne Jolliffe, interviewed by Catherine Lackner, March 30, 1998. Transcript: p. 13.

44. Fred Allardyce, interviewed by Catherine Lackner, April 8, 1998. Transcript: p. 19.

45. *The New York Times*, March 2, 1990: D, p. 4.

46. *Financial World*, May 25, 1995.

47. American Standard 1993 press release.

48. Gary Brogoch, interviewed by Catherine Lackner, April 2, 1998. Transcript: p. 6.

49. George Kerckhove, interviewed by the author, November 20, 1997. Transcript: p. 26.

50. "American Standard Companies Inc. Holds First Annual Meeting," PR Newswire, Inc., May 4, 1995.

51. "The New America," *Investor's Business Daily*, February 8, 1995.

52. 1995 American Standard annual report: p. 2.

53. *Ibid.*, cover.
54. *The New York Times*, December 18, 1996: p. 4.
55. American Standard news release, March 10, 1997.
56. Allardyce interview, transcript: p. 5.
57. Janet Murnick, interviewed by Alex Lieber, April 15, 1998. Transcript: p. 5.
58. Judith Britz, interviewed by Catherine Lackner, April 6, 1998. Transcript: p. 9.
59. *Ibid.*

60. Luigi Gandini, interviewed by Catherine Lackner, April 2, 1998. Transcript: p. 11.
61. Kampouris interview, transcript: p. 17.
62. Horst Hinrichs, interviewed by the author, November 20, 1997. Transcript: p. 19.
63. Wolfgang Voss, interviewed by Alex Lieber, April 15, 1998. Transcript: p. 6.
64. Wilfried Delker, interviewed by Catherine Lackner, April 3, 1998. Transcript: p. 5.

65. "American Standard Companies, Inc. Reports 17 percent increase in Earnings Per Share," company news release, February 3, 1998.
66. "The Man Who Puts Working Capital To Work," *Chief Executive*, October 1996.

Chapter Twelve Sidebar

1. Emmanuel Kampouris, interviewed by Alex Lieber, December 22, 1998. Transcript: p. 18.

INDEX